Europe Beyond Your Means

Europe Beyond Your Means

✦

The Paris Edition

Conrad Lucas II

&

William D. Norgard

iUniverse, Inc.
New York   Bloomington

Europe Beyond Your Means
The Paris Edition

iUniverse books may be ordered through booksellers or by contacting:

iUniverse
1663 Liberty Drive
Bloomington, IN 47403
www.iuniverse.com
1-800-Authors (1-800-288-4677)

ISBN: 978-0-595-47927-6 (pbk)
ISBN: 978-0-595-71605-0 (cloth)
ISBN: 978-1-4401-1599-8 (ebk)

Printed in the United States of America

iUniverse rev. date: 12/12/2008

"Anyone who lives within their means suffers from a lack of imagination."

—Oscar Wilde

To

Jody, Trish, Dave, & Nancy

Thanks for living within your means so we could live beyond ours.

Contents

Welcome to
Europe Beyond Your Means

Bookshelves today are crowded with titles that give the same advice, recommend the same places to visit, and ultimately convey the philosophy that travel should be brief, cursory, and cheap. *Europe Beyond Your Means* is the work of two writers hoping to exploit what they see as a dearth in the tourist reading market. Consider this the introduction of a totally new genre that exists as a supplement for the discerning traveler who isn't looking for prepackaged travel tips but instead craves social commentary and permission to break from the norm and discard the fanny pack.

While invoking our particular brand of social justice, we have produced a book filled with political satire, short stories, humorous observations, bar crawls, and offhand but fairly obvious travel and appearance tips. The overall goal of this publication is to act as a guide for those lost souls who feel unaccounted for by the typical travel literature on the market today, while debunking certain engrained stereotypes. This book exists because we feel there need to be statutes for *Beyond Your Means Travelers* to follow and cite when others are spotted violating what should undoubtedly be a solid body of established international law. This is, in short, a reaction to other travel books—a "tra-vella," if you will.

The question looms: Who exactly was this book prepared for and who are *Beyond Your Means* travelers? In short, these are the pseudo-intellectual spendthrifts that regular tourists often see but rarely engage when wandering with tour groups, for fear of dishonoring the "buddy system." Essentially, if you can identify with the following scenario, you, too, may be a *Beyond Your Means* traveler:

It's the beginning of a particularly trying time at work or school, and many important deadlines are approaching. Conventional wisdom holds that if energy is directed toward the tasks at hand, the rewards themselves will be so immense as to make the exertion seem minuscule. Instead of staying up all hours slaving away on work-related projects, you pass the time by checking international news sources on the Web, worrying if your dry cleaning will be done by the weekend, and investing energy in planning an exotic trip with money you don't have. By championing this *unique* ideology, you have moved in the direction of becoming a true *Beyond Your Means* traveler.

These travelers have a strong distaste for the contents of most travel guides and are disenfranchised by the many ill-suited suggestions aimed at the mainstream. For some reason unbeknownst to your authors, the world just doesn't quite embrace the *Beyond Your Means* lifestyle. The typical travel guide will steer readers away from enticement and toward the direction of the bland, while lulling them to sleep with boring facts rather than highlighting the rich, idiosyncratic history of a place and its people. This may very well be the credo for the masses—but not for a *Beyond Your Means* philosopher.

A myriad of travel information currently focuses on how to plan an economically conscious trip to an interesting locale and how to fit as many highlights into as few days as possible. But we don't believe that meaningful travel experiences can—or should—always be bought at deep discounts while lodging in hostile environments. Another disappointing theme recurring in standard travel guide parlance is the emphasis on Disneyland-style casual dress. The prevailing paradigm of the modern era is that travel is best accomplished in a pair of Nikes and white athletic socks, in hopes of saving a trip to the podiatrist some day. All of this well-heeled advice is bought and sold at the price of looking derelict in some of Europe's most public and celebrated places. One might have won the war for comfort but sacrificed a great deal of class in doing it. This is nothing but the most Pyrrhic of victories under false accords. After all, Wal-Mart is a lovely idea for toilet paper and household cleaning supplies, but it's not the philosophy to employ when your quest is sipping Chablis on the *Champs-Élysées*. If you're constantly worried about paying for tomorrow, you'll forget what you can later regret spending today.

Contained herewith is not a step-by-step guide to your next escape to Europe; this isn't that kind of publication. Our aim isn't to be your number one resource for vacation tips but instead to create the antithesis to the "common" travel guide. We keep the "in-the-knows" entertained and the *poseurs des normes* obvious. We're not writing a nauseating Rick Steves hand-holding manifesto, telling you all the details of budget travel. If you stick with us, you won't be spotted walking through a train station, wearing a backpack on the front of your chest laden with locks, like the Ghost of Christmas Past. Efforts like those make you nothing but a rank-and-file member of the "Ricknick" army. We, on the other hand, tell you the stuff Rick didn't think about or warned you against because of the "frivolous" cost.

The bottom line of the *Beyond Your Means* philosophy is simple: life is lived and best enjoyed when experiencing and striving for what you don't yet have but think you already should.

Conrad G. Lucas II	William D. Norgard
New Orleans, Louisiana	New York, New York

1

Introduction: Who Are Beyond Your Means Travelers?

Beyond Your Means travelers are varied in their differing approaches to life. Perhaps the one common denominator is a true passion for living life to the fullest at any given opportunity. Many practitioners don't necessarily associate with one another because the only unifying trait among them is financial irresponsibility or the disdain for securing gainful employment. Each lives the *Beyond Your Means* lifestyle on his or her own terms, but in the spirit of Maslow's hierarchy, self-actualization is the goal that allows each traveler to fully embrace an individual niche.

It is also important to understand which approach to take before boarding the plane. This can have vast implications concerning 1) the justification for your vacation, 2) realizing your actual motives, and 3) your subsequent packing. Such an individualized approach to traveling comes with the caveat that certain traits are only exhibited while living in the fantasy world of travel abroad. *Beyond Your Means* travelers, however, are often stuck in a state of alternate reality and may occasionally exhibit these traits domestically—much to the chagrin of their comrades.

There are varying interpretations of the categories that *Beyond Your Means* travelers fall into, but the following are some of the more classic examples:

Artistic/Writer Type

This is a very broad category for *Beyond Your Means* travelers, as it includes those who hopelessly romanticize the ex-pat lifestyle and long for yesteryear, while overlooking the operative word, "fiction," in "historical fiction." These particular individuals love nothing more than sitting at Parisian cafés and using a verbally baroque style to philosophize about world issues or whatever may tickle their proverbial fancy. In Paris, they might proudly adorn their heads with berets and their faces with sly smirks, while forgetting their car payments awaiting them back home. They've been telling their friends for years about a book idea they are supposedly perfecting, but in Paris, they unsolicitedly share with other café patrons that their many books have already been published, only under a secretive *nom de plume*.

Jet-Setter

In the mind of this particular traveler, descendants of European royalty or the children of Arab oil barons could, at any given time, recognize him on the *rue* as one of their own—or at least ponder where they have seen him before. Always wearing black designer sunglasses and a black coat, he isn't above calling an exclusive bar and asking for a private entrance for "security purposes." The realization that Prince William doesn't have him on speed dial is easily forgotten during a stint in any glitzy international city, especially Paris.

Professional Nomad

A professional nomad likely lives a *Beyond Your Means* lifestyle just about everywhere because no location is ever home for very long. This is the kind of person whose life is always an adventure as he moves around the world for various jobs or other reasons. Once the local restaurant selection grows tiring, he moves. A professional nomad can easily reconcile his expensive travel habits with his inadequate income under the guise of a "you only live once" philosophy. Considering that numerous creditors and relatives have all but taken a hit out on them, changing addresses frequently is not always a bad idea.

Aging Collegiate Who Can't Let Go

Inside every *Beyond Your Means* traveler exists the spirit of a fifth-year senior who just isn't quite ready to grow-up. For some travelers, this is the driving personality that leads to drinking binges and decisions generally reserved for twenty-year-olds. Despite age or adult situations, some travelers are still dominated by their inner frat boy. A special quality reserved for this type of traveler is having the fortitude to resist the criticism of friends who continually encourage him to "grow up" or "leave those days behind." He also is known to enjoy watching the sunrise on the Seine each morning, not as part of a romantic interlude but because he doesn't have the frame of mind to remember where he is staying.

The One-Timer

While it is contrary to the general principles of *Beyond Your Means* traveling, there are those who strive to take a vacation to Paris using this prescribed methodology only once. This individual is more acceptable to society, as she doesn't continually find reasons to make irresponsible decisions, but when traveling, she isn't part of the typical categories. A pure *Beyond Your Means* traveler spits in the face of bourgeois prejudices, but the "one-timer" tries not to rock the boat too much. By and large, the one-timer will use this trip as a capstone to an event in life or an appropriate interlude between life phases. Quite dissimilar to the *Beyond Your Means* archetype, a one-timer will habitually be honest about her life at home and see no need to take poetic license when entertaining others with tales of forthcoming novels or diplomatic connections.

Raison d'être

While the idea of voyaging to France is something understandable to the masses, traveling in the *Beyond Your Means* fashion may seem strange to those without this peculiar perspective. A *Beyond Your Means* traveler often needs little reason or excuse to personally justify quitting a job or putting life on hold to live in the City of Lights. Not everyone, however, understands this approach. Considering that many travel guides assume that readers' general priorities are career and future, rather than leisure and decadence, it is necessary to rationalize seemingly poor decisions to family and friends in terms they can respect. Since most are not able to grasp the *je ne sais quoi* of spending a month in Paris, it is important to develop alternate reasons to articulate to those who are so quick to condemn.

The suggestions given here can be easily adapted, depending on the situation of the traveler. For example, a recent college graduate has much more leverage than a thirty-five-year-old in claiming a need to satisfy a lifelong wanderlust. In developing a plan utilizing spin-filled communication to share with the rest of the world, these suggestions will help you develop your own personal rationale and tailor our recommendations to your current station in life.

Cultural and Historical Value

First and foremost, a traveler can always rationalize a trip to Paris based on cultural and historical value. This excuse is indisputably understood by those easily fooled. If this is a traveler's first trip to Paris, then very little explanation is necessary, as the cultural value of the city is apparent. Any traveler will be hard pressed to find an individual who argues that visiting Paris for at least some amount of time is not culturally beneficial. Be sure to frame the cultural and historical arguments appropriately. Anything is better than revealing your real cultural exploration, which consists of spending borrowed money at trendy bars.

"Finding Oneself"

This ubiquitous concept has always had such a great ring that it easily supports itself, despite having no real meaning. It is highly possible that stating that the goal of your trip is to "find myself" will garner a smile and a look of understanding from others who likely think you are lost. To find oneself is curiously respected by all who have never wasted thousands of dollars living the high life in a foreign country. Those who can't comprehend such a frivolous lifestyle accept this excuse because they don't know that a *Beyond Your Means* traveler can't locate this elusive ideal any better in Paris than in Hoboken. Despite a traveler's age or stock in life, finding oneself is always acceptable to some—spouses and employers being prominent exceptions. However, if there have been previous "finding" adventures throughout the years, a *Beyond Your Means* traveler may have to resort to citing the furtherance of specific business or education goals.

Résumé Building

The last thing on the mind of many travelers may be career planning, but the fact is that the world places high value on this endeavor. For many *Beyond Your Means* travelers, the enemy is adult responsibility. Thus, it is important to heed the advice of Sun Tzu and "know thine enemy." Again, depending on the traveler's age and position, this set of reasons can take on various incarnations.

Case in point, a law student can profess a passion for international law and locate a study-abroad program. There is such a tradition of foreigners studying in Paris that locating a program for college, law, business, or virtually anything else proves fairly easy. However, if the days of higher education have long since passed, there are still a number of French-language-immersion and international business programs in which a *Beyond Your Means* traveler can enroll for the stated reasons of improving his personal marketability.

Ultimately, others like to hear about the end result of such elaborate ventures; thus, anything that can be phrased as improving career prospects will earn instant credibility. Still, those hearing this reason might already be skeptical about the actual motivation, so perhaps it is best to choose another path that at least meshes better with your personality.

One Last Hurrah

Considering a *Beyond Your Means* traveler's likely history, this reason will be more believable than the sudden onset of responsible thinking and planning for an adult career. Those who know you may accept the "one last hurrah" as the last adventure before growing up and doing things differently. Using this excuse involves a few months of preparation by telling friends and relatives of a desire to mature. After promulgating such a position over a period of time, it is then acceptable to share the final plans for eliminating the last remaining vestiges of irresponsibility still latent in your system.

This excuse perhaps works best when preceding a landmark event in life, such as a wedding or a milestone birthday. Because of the very nature of the excuse itself, it should be used sparingly or else it will be dismissed—and for good reason.

Whatever particular communications strategy is employed, these suggestions can be useful. Ultimately, you know your audience better than anyone, and so you should carefully plan to ensure success.

Choosing Travel Companions

When planning a vacation that lasts longer than a week, choosing the right travel companions is key. It is difficult to travel *Beyond Your Means* without others around to inspire irresponsible decisions and the type of indulgence necessary to live up to your own lofty expectations. There are general factors to consider, along with certain specifics, that will ensure a great trip for all involved and remind the folks at Visa and MasterCard why you are one of their favorite clients. First and foremost, avoiding those with a total group mentality is a must. The ideal travel group consists of several people, each playing a different role to complete the experience. Depending on the number willing to embark on such an extended vacation to Paris, certain roles can be dovetailed into one another.

The Other *Beyond Your Means* Traveler(s)

For a vacation in Paris to be a completely irresponsible experience, at least one of the other members in the group must be a fellow *Beyond Your Means* practitioner. This is the person who will constantly help push you to new and exciting limits and will never back down from a challenge. It is important to enjoy one another's company, but perhaps it's even more important to have a mutual understanding—neither of you will ever retreat from tilt and tourney, regardless of how badly your bodies and bank accounts need to recover from a few too many nights out. Depending on the size of your travel group, this will be your fellow advocate for ridiculous propositions. It is too easy for other group members to dismiss and isolate one *Beyond Your Means* traveler, but multiple *Beyond Your Means* travelers may be too much to keep the flames of extravagance from catching fire.

The Cheap One

The concept of traveling *Beyond Your Means* is that your means don't match the lifestyle you lead. This unfortunate reality is something that *Beyond Your Means* theorists must confront, but it is best to allow a fellow traveler who practices frugality to be the person to suggest that individual king-sized feather beds aren't necessary. Subtly working with this person enhances the social cachet of *Beyond Your Means* philosophers. The miser takes the blame for certain things not coming to fruition, while *Beyond Your Means* travelers can continue to make irresponsible suggestions without actually having to follow through with them.

The Polyglot

Ideally, this individual serves a greater role than just vast linguistic knowledge, but having someone with a command of the French language is essential. The faulty conventional wisdom among many "Ricknicks" and others is that everyone in France knows English. While many French are impressively multilingual, being armed with a Francophone at your side helps when traveling outside of major cities or when engaging in late-night arguments with cab drivers. There is a great possibility that when spending time in Paris, knowledge of the language will be vital. Imagine a scenario where a traveler needs to locate a department store and, specifically, buy a three-pronged converter. Basically, knowing French is helpful. Anyone who has ever asked for strawberry "*préservatifs*" with their croissant understands why. (*Préservatifs* is a false cognate since in French the term means prophylactics rather than jam.)

The Return-Ticket Holder

A difficult realization for *Beyond Your Means* travelers is that eventually a vacation must end. Because many of these philosophers often live their lives in an alternate version of reality, returning home may be difficult. Also, sometimes in order to free up a month or a summer for such an excursion, a *Beyond Your Means* traveler may have whimsically quit a job, gotten fired, or just disappeared. Therefore, a travel companion who has an actual reason to return home is indispensable. The reasons themselves may range from work to school to family obligations, but without this individual, there is no telling how long a *Beyond Your Means* traveler could be gone or how much money will be spent.

Add-Ons

If each of the aforementioned roles has been filled, then any additional members on the trip must occupy what is arguably the most important role of all: These individuals become the audience for the many stories offered by the *Beyond Your Means* travelers, and they serve as a posse to feed the endless egos of the group leaders.

In addition, add-ons who have never been to Paris can also provide the necessary motivation to visit some of the cultural sites that other group travelers may consider "touristy." In terms of numbers, it boils down to an individual decision. There is something to be said for limiting the number of add-ons for logistical purposes, but after careful deliberation, the best recommendation to be offered is the more the merrier. On the nights when complete domination of a bar or club is necessary, the larger the group is, the easier it is to accomplish the task at hand.

2

Understanding France

The question asks itself: why France and why Paris? The answer is obvious, because there isn't any country or locale in the world that epitomizes the *Beyond Your Means* philosophy more than the land that gave us *haute couture*. The French do everything to the extreme. No people in the world devote more to the celebration of themselves, their culture, or the ordinary aspects of daily life than the French. Along the banks of the Seine, the very notion of having a meal with just one or two courses would force any true Parisian into an epileptic fit. With every spray of specially blended *eau de toilette*, Jacques and Pierre embark on a time-honored cultural ritual full of affectations that draw curiosity from onlookers across the globe. Essentially, pretension is not a negative personal characteristic to the French—it's an innate right.

So the question looms, why is it that the French are known throughout the world as the icons of culture and beauty? France's position as the Mecca for culture and beauty is certainly not *nouveau*. Coco Chanel's little black dress and other French creations evolved from a long line of forays into decadent fashions. Take male formal dress, for instance; while the modern suit follows a Victorian pattern, its roots go back to the court of Louis XIV, the Sun King. A flamboyant dresser, Louis insisted that his courtiers wear a long coat, waistcoat, cravat, and breeches. The French were the last real Western society to hold onto the notion that men should be dressed equally as—or even more—beautifully than women. The Royal Peacock was so interested in making men's clothing every bit as fancy and fussy as women's clothes that he could have made Liberace look like nothing more than a curiosity at the local county fair.

It was not until the French Revolution that simplicity in clothing eclipsed the elaborate designs of the previous era. This period can be looked at as being the eighteenth-century precursor of the Seattle grunge look, but at least *they* could blame a revolution. This being France, it didn't take very long for this briefly chic look to go back out of style—social equality is as natural to the French as McDonald's selling Beluga Caviar Extra-Value Meals.

Today, the French can be quite meticulous when accessorizing their mode of dress. Both men and women often don neatly shined shoes and pressed pants. While bright colors might be considered unusual or even gaudy to some North Americans, they attract positive attention in France. After all, it's called "French Blue" for a reason. The color attracts notice, while providing an air of wealth and prestige equivalent to a Connecticut spring bride serving at a homeless shelter in Newark.

Relating to the French passion for fashion is the enduring French fashion of passion. The French seem to constantly be in love, think about love, write or paint about love, or lament the absence of a once great love. Culturally speaking, the French may have a slightly different perception of *amour* than most places. Love in France seems to be as constant as it is fitful and as permanent as it is temporary.

Unlike puritanical nations—the United States, for instance—the French find it much more acceptable to succumb to personal lusts and desires. Surrendering to the passions of the heart is artistically beautiful, rather than selfishly shameful. The fulfillment of a great desire is viewed as positive, while abstention is considered harmful. The French populace loves to feel seduced, as well as loving to beguile one another. Seduction is, without any doubt, the highest social art in France and does not always have to be of a sexual nature. There is no greater political compliment in France than to be labeled a *seductuer*. This is normally paid to someone with a wink, a nod, and a smile, rather than being one of many insults in a heated conversation. Seduction is a skill exalted by the French, with regard to a politician's relation to the populace, and is also admired in the affairs of the heart, irrespective of the bonds of marriage.

Parisians can be said to not only accept promiscuity but to almost encourage it. During the 1980s, French president François Mitterrand engaged in several extramarital affairs and kept one well-known mistress, who was 27 years his junior. Many in the French public looked approvingly on the behavior, as it proved to them that the old man still had plenty of virility and magnetic grace left. If the majority of the country doesn't seem to care that the president is having affairs, then it hardly makes it a competitive sport for investigative journalism. Hence, Mitterrand was even able to support an illegitimate daughter the whole time he was in office without much interference from the press corps. The fact that he was capable of seducing many younger women while in the Élysée Palace only made him that much more attractive as a candidate to the voters of France. An interesting twist to the end of the story that highlights the French acceptance of extramarital affairs is that Mitterrand's "other family" was invited to his funeral in 1996 and seated next to his legitimate one.

As further evidence of the French obsession with seduction at even the highest levels of culture, take the depiction of their national symbol, *la Marianne*. Even she, the most esteemed image in the French nation, has gotten in on the act. Intended to personify Liberty and Reason, she is regularly depicted as a callipygian character, in tattered clothes and provocative poses, with her ample bosom exposed. This is essentially a very French approach, as it proves difficult to imagine Uncle Sam as a septuagenarian sexual object. Maybe the French have it right and the Americans wrong. Uncle Sam, while appearing steadfast and stalwart, seems to always be asking for something ("I Want You!") while *Marianne* seems to be offering something we all want (this you can figure out for yourself). Either way it is analyzed, the French seem to be undeniably implying that a healthy libido does not necessarily need to be suppressed, even when occupying the nation's highest office or symbolically embodying its spirit.

Following suit, there also seems to be an acceptance of the young mistress in Paris, unlike anywhere else in the world. Most Parisians would not think twice about a short-lived love affair between a young woman and a married man thirty years her senior. It is simply considered normal and assumed that an older man has the necessary experience to finally be a great lover, because by that time, he has become a recipient of doctoral letters in the field of seduction. Thus, the affair can take on more of a professorial quality than what she might be accustomed to in her peer group. Keeping a mistress is just expected by many in French society. The husband's actions are looked at as "behaving badly," rather than actually intending to destroy the marriage. He is eventually expected to end his torrid affair and accept his fate as already married in the end.

This approach carries over to the French views on commitment of all forms. French females are notorious for constantly having a boyfriend (*petit ami*), although there might be a misunderstanding in the English sense of the word "boyfriend"—this normally would denote the public acknowledgement of a monogamous relationship. In France, however, going on one or two dates can equate to being a *petit ami*. Exchanging a phone number with perceived future intent might have the same result. And having one *petit ami* does not mean someone cannot have more. In fact, it is not uncommon for French women to maintain up to four *petits amis* at one time. To be fair, this does not automatically denote a relationship of a sexual nature. Obviously, the kind of woman who has these relationships is relevant. Saying that you have no *petits amis* appears to be more of a negative social stigma than having more than one. It might be like admitting that you are personally lacking in the faculty of seduction—the French equivalent to a large goiter on the neck. Therefore, as a man, if a potential interest tells you that she has a *petit ami*, it should not be necessarily viewed as rejection. On the contrary, it may just be that your femme fatale requires a little pursuit before she will count you among her other *petits amis*.

French men rarely claim to have a *petite amie,* and if they do, they stress the lack of seriousness or formality in the relationship. Some things are the same no matter what country you live in.

High-School Diplomacy in the Western World

France is a unique and individualist persona on the world stage. Any student of political science is quite aware that the complexities that surround international relations can take volumes to fully understand. Many a scholar has written on the internal differences that exist within the Western world, but those works, while highly credible, may be a bit too much to digest prior to planning a journey where the overall goal may be much less complicated. But a *Beyond Your Means* traveler prefers to have a well-informed opinion about a place and its people before a visit; therefore, it is appropriate to summarize thousands of pages written on diplomacy by looking at the Western world and France's role through a lens with that we can all appreciate: *high school.*

The picture is all too familiar: it's early morning in any typical suburban high school. Prior to the day's orientation period or "homeroom," as it may be known, students are situated throughout the class, perhaps eating muffins or sipping on their beverages of choice. The conversation circles that form are enough to make a professor of human behavior salivate. Yes, there are cliques and groups that are in natural opposition. A spitball may be thrown from one table to another as a warning or a threat, much like a nuclear test may be held in the diplomatic world.

About fifteen minutes before the bell rings and the reading of morning announcements sound, a familiar character sits atop a desk, pontificating, while a crowd gathers around. In the Western world, this character is the United States. He sits proudly, wearing a letterman jacket and regaling anyone within earshot of recent big-game triumphs. Others sit in awe. The United States isn't an exclusive character, despite his apropos all-American look. He was raised in a good family, with parents of humble means who did well for themselves His parents instilled in him certain non-discriminating values; thus, all are welcome to attend his daily homeroom speech, suggesting he is more "salt of the earth" in his social associations. Because of the United States' accomplishments, or in spite of them, he is now far from humble. Still, he acknowledges everyone equally when in the school setting, despite their financial resources or those with whom he associates on the weekends.

Always at his side, decked out in a cardigan or some plaid accessory, is England. He's ready and willing to defend the United States, when others may be passing notes or plotting temporary revolts to his social dominance. England is also a valuable resource, as he is always well prepared with any number of course outlines and the Latin notes to help the United States on midterm exams. England is always ready to laugh a little too hard at a joke that falls flat or offer a prompting line to remind the United States of an appropriate story that could be a gap-filler. The ten or fifteen other countries sitting around the table, some enjoying government-subsidized milk, chuckle appropriately when necessary.

At the back of the room, alone, sits Russia. He's a rather large and imposing figure and is also a valued member of the football team, as the school's premier defensive lineman and record holder in sacks and tackles. When he is on his game, he helps tremendously, but sometimes in the middle of a playoff or state championship, he launches into an internal tirade, rendering him largely ineffective. In the mornings before homeroom, Russia often sits staring intently at something. The United States is always cordial, and England follows suit, but everyone is a bit leery because in junior high, Russia brought a gun to school and had to go away for awhile. But he's back, and everyone has been willing to give him a chance. Lately, however, he is showing signs of returning to his old ways, and rumor has it that the guidance counselor is involved. This can't be verified, but every day during health class, he gets a special pass to leave to be an "office helper."

Near Russia, toward the back of the room, sits China. Despite their seating proximity, they haven't really been friends since Russia returned to the school system. China is intent in doing well in any and all math and science classes. He is a shifty character, who thinks that none of the other nations are on to his plans of eventual domination and destruction of the high school, but those facts are assumed by the popular crowd. No one has ever seen China's parents, and there is a rumor that he lives at the orphanage in town. He arrives at school by 6:00 a.m. and does not leave until the building closes. He spends his time in the library and roaming the halls, carefully taking notes on everything, regardless of whether the information is useful.

Sitting front and center, not only in homeroom but in every other class, is a good-looking and diligent student, Germany. He comes from a single-family household, where he is the oldest brother in a large family. His father walked out on them years ago, so he was forced to assume the role of adult male quite early on in life. Despite this, Germany has excelled in every subject and every objective that has been set out for him, aside from socially. He dismisses the United States and England as inferior because he is not only the best member of the football team, but he also takes all advanced placement classes and carries a 4.1 grade point average. He is still smarting from his B+ in literature. England got an A. Germany cannot understand why the other countries would follow anyone but him. Because of this, he is unable to engage in locker-room banter with the others, as he takes the lighthearted criticism too harshly. He is well known for his ruthless temper; thus, his role with the United States and England is often reduced to a mutual head nod in the hallway or the occasional "good game" acknowledgment.

As the bell rings and the students disperse to their assigned seats, the teacher begins to take role. The room is quiet, and everyone is obedient. The United States sits with a pleasant smile on his face, England gathers all of his books for the day, and Germany tries to ensure a perfectly sharp point on each of his pencils. China stares and takes notes.

About ten minutes into the announcements, a female—perhaps the most enticing and best dressed in the history of the entire school—bursts through the door. She is always on the homecoming court and has fashions that are too cutting-edge for a seventeen-year-old. In her hand she carries a double latte, indicating not only that arriving at school on time is not a priority, but also that she is far too sophisticated to drink milk or orange juice in her late teenage years. Long ago she decided that the school's no-smoking policy did not apply to her, so she never leaves home without an elegant cigarette case tucked away in her Louis Vuitton. This beautiful *pièce de résistance* is none other than France.

France sits at the front of the room and speaks to no one, but all the boys stare in awe. Her beauty is as intriguing as her wealth—after all, her dad did fund the new cheerleading uniforms. England has had a crush on her for years but would never ask her out and has been reduced to just making fun of her to placate himself. France's beauty and dismissive demeanor have taught her that she can get what she wants, despite her cavalier approach to school. Occasionally, however, her father threatens to take away her valued possessions if her grades don't improve. There was a memorable event at the end of junior year when her red convertible was at risk. As a result, France shockingly came to school prepared with notes, hired a special tutor, and subsequently set the curve in her Western Civilization class. After securing her ownership of the car, she wasn't seen at school again for at least a month.

Her relations with other nations have always been a bit difficult, as it is hard to find someone willing to handle her mood swings. France and the United States dated in the past, but it didn't work out. They had that one hot summer between freshman and sophomore years but never dated during the actual school year. After the fleeting affair with the United States, France's father suggested that she date Germany during her junior year. At first, France was reluctant, citing the excuse that they had nothing in common, but France's father reminded her that Germany was hard working and bound to be successful, so she should at least give him a chance. She acquiesced. On their first date, Germany took France to a carnival and won her a goldfish on his first try. This goldfish was to be their mutual pet named Alsace. Things between Germany and France never truly stabilized after their first few dates, and a bitter verbal battle ensued on who should actually keep Alsace. This went on for a while until one weekend, while everyone was at the same party, France decided to tell Germany formally that she wanted to see other nations …Germany hit her.

Everyone else was forced to get involved. In the end, France got to keep the fish. At present, all the other nations are leery whenever Germany and France are in the same room because Germany's interest in striking France again is perpetually looming. The United States and England, friends from the womb, have privately determined that France should be "put in her place" because of her better-than-you attitude, but they always restrain Germany. Lately, however, Germany helped France prepare an outline for their economics study group, and relations between the two have warmed.

No matter how far one goes in life, high school is never too far behind. In some way, everyone has a seat at the table, even France's attractive cousin who lives in another town, Italy, and the quirky lovechild between England's mom and France's dad, who lives next to the United States, Canada. Understanding these dynamics, which are essential to world travel or engaging in political discussion with friends from across the globe, can be made easier by reducing everything to what we know best.

Bi-Polar Nation

The French idea of democracy also seems radically different at first blush, when compared to their Western brethrens'. French approaches to government often feel like ideas written on a napkin during a sloppy drunken affair, with the spirit of the revolution accurately described as a full-fledged hangover. So much social unrest could never be caused by anyone who wasn't at least a little bit tipsy. They have undergone numerous revolutions since 1789, with the general mood over the years trending more and more toward outright socialism. After a few too many Kronenbergs, even that can seem like a good idea. This was all rolling along quite smoothly for the French until they tried to push a little too hard to the left in May 1968. De Gaulle, acting very much like the designated driver, stopped this from becoming a full-blown revolution (again) by labeling the rioters "Communists," which reversed sympathies toward the "revolutionaries" in the mind of the populace. It follows that the French don't really mind standing shoulder-to-shoulder with Trotsky, but they really would prefer to be on his right. Recent elections in France indicate that the nation is still as split as ever but has at least turned in the direction of capitalism.

The structure of French politics and politicians alone is enough to divert the attention of even the most extreme conspiracy theorists. Politics in France is really rather simple. If accepted to *Science Po* or *École Nationale d'Administration*, you earn a spot in the French social club that is the government. A politico can be wildly unpopular or totally inept at a job but will still garner appointments to cushy governmental positions, occupy minister housing in central Paris, and work in ornate buildings that put their institutional-looking American counterparts to shame. Unpopular politicians can be removed from their positions, but when their atrocities start to fade from the press and the plebian mind, they are reinserted elsewhere in government. It's an endless cycle of political favors and elitism. In some ways, *fraternité* is reserved for a few at the top.

In terms of modern politics, French politicians are expected to listen carefully and abide by the will of the people. But essentially, they operate a patriarchal state, making decisions that, in the end, at least flirt with notions of common sense and economic stewardship. Some might say it is an appropriate metaphor to view the French people as wayward teenagers, screaming for social change. After all, the French do love to riot. But their leaders have been accused of possessing no real intention of doing anything except paying the masses empty lip service. The proletariat can often make a lot of noise, while blathering on about unreachable social goals and ideals that make no practical or logical sense in a modern market economy. It might, though, after a bottle of Moët & Chandon.

All this leads to a famous Gallic dichotomy: the French, in thought, versus the French, in practice. When polled in 2006, only 36 percent of the French thought that a free-market economy was the best available system. France, however, exhibits all of the same—if not more—overindulgences of any other Western nation, with Paris acting as an epicenter of the country's—if not the world's—capitalistic excesses. Saying that the French are socialists is like calling Hooters a reputable establishment merely because it has Dom Pérignon on the menu.

Some of this "contrary to actual practice" thinking seems to be taught in the schools. Of the three main *baccalauréat* (high school) options, one translates roughly into "economic and social science." A widely used textbook in this subject devotes page after page to Marxist theories of production, class struggle, and bourgeois exploitation. In a section on the labor market, it states that "employers seek to divide workers in order to reduce solidarity between different categories of staff." French psychosis, then, is no surprise, considering that they teach Communist propaganda in their high schools but at the same time require their citizens to be up-to-date on the newest trends and expensive perfumes. So, in short, they view Marxist philosophy as plausibly correct but the principles of Givenchy as pretty credible, too.

Despite its temperamental political nature and history, France has remained a world power since time immemorial and a favorite destination of globe-trotters for generations. With all the quixotic tendencies of her people, France is endlessly fascinating and full of treasured locations, providing ample opportunity to engage in the types of activities that *Beyond Your Means* travelers value. A true overview of French politics and life is best developed from extensive observations; hence, a *Beyond Your Means* traveler should spend as much time as possible among the French to understand them better. Therefore, spending your life's savings on champagne and caviar can easily be justified as political research. Finding ways to explain this reason to friends and co-workers is best left to the next section.

How to Use This Book

As you have may have noticed by now, the *Europe Beyond Your Means* philosophical strengths lie in sweeping generalizations on complex topics. As such, this book is best utilized as an overarching social-concept map, as opposed to an encyclopedic list of restaurants, sights, and other attractions. Your authors recommend reading the text as you would any other literary masterpiece, thus engaging the total thesis rather than spot-checking for specific information. That being said, several recommendations and "must sees" are scattered throughout the book and in the index, as these are places that we frequented and thoroughly enjoyed. Basically, reading *Europe Beyond Your Means* should be the equivalent experience to reading Thoreau, because while he does recommend visiting a specific pond, the overall goal really is an artistic journey.

3

Planning Your Trip

✦

Duration of the Journey

How long does one have to remain in a place before claiming to have lived there? When is it apropos to describe a short vacation as a jaunt? Both are questions that many *Beyond Your Means travelers* ask themselves. Answers to these elusive inquiries may very well turn on the relationship you have with trivial things, like your job or your financial resources. Fear not, however, because any limitations you might be forced to accept or endure can easily be spun into provocative tales of adventure and alleged intemperance. Generally, most travelers will plan a week or even less in the world's cultural capital, but in order to truly get to know the place and speak with any authority, a much longer stay may be in order.

It is possible to learn the city rather quickly, if necessary, and make classic generic comments like, "There was this little café in the 4th I just adored" to convince others that you really immersed yourself. Enough souls have been to Paris that you may need to provide more specific details about your cultural immersion. Providing names like *"Chez Jacques"* in "Montmartre," where you had great *"café au lait"* served by a waitress named *"Sophie"* may lead to some skepticism. Basically, spending a longer amount of time in Paris will provide ample opportunity to establish a routine and possibly convince yourself and others that you really are an ex-pat. Details make a story better.

Most *Beyond Your Means* travelers have a much lower threshold than the average person for the amount of time it takes to claim residency in a particular locale. While there is no objective standard for the length of time required before calling somewhere "home," there are certain norms that are generally observed. Typically, one cannot claim to have "lived" somewhere unless he remains for at least three months or uses a seasonal period, like "the summer," as a qualifier. However, many *Beyond Your Means* travelers are known to have embellished the amount of time spent in Paris—and elsewhere—to seem more worldly. While this is not discouraged, keep in mind that the longer you supposedly lived in a location, the better handle you should have on a city and its people. For example, if you claim to have lived in Paris for a year, odds are that you will be expected to have French friends and discuss a vast array of experiences. Therefore, stretching a short trip for Bastille Day into a six-month sojourner must be done with absolute caution. Additionally, the more time spent abroad, the more of the language a traveler should know. People will expect you to translate short phrases, and simply making them up will not fool many for very long. The duty of the authors is simply to warn what might happen if a story is stretched too far.

Most *Beyond Your Means* travelers laugh in the face of obligations, so that will not normally affect the duration of a sabbatical. But if travel companions are involved, or if the almighty dollar has been stretched to its absolute limits, then avoiding a cliché "pros and cons" list will be nearly impossible. Thus, while a longer trip is strongly recommended, a shorter trip is also beneficial and might be more manageable to your particular situation.

Short Trip

Being able to say "When I lived in Paris" has an equal amount of social cachet later in life as being able to mention "I'm just going to pop over to Paris for the weekend" does today. There is perhaps no other phrase in all of travel parlance that incites more envy. While at first it may seem that taking a short trip is prima facie contradictory to the Beyond Your Means lifestyle, that is not necessarily the case. During a short trip, a traveler is less likely to be required to budget for a long period of time and can spend ridiculous amounts of money enjoying life's simple pleasures. Regardless of the length of time you'll be staying, there is a certain verbal currency associated with any trip to the city sur la Seine.

Nevertheless, an abbreviated jaunt to Paris has its own unique set of considerations in terms of lodging, as it may not be practical to rent an apartment for a few days. Therefore, heed these warnings:

Hostels

The mistake that too many travelers make when going to the City of Lights is to follow the suggestions of a travel guide (that is, other travel guides) and stay in a hostel. For purposes of this book, the spelling will be changed to "hostile," because that is more accurate. Yes, there may be something to be said for traveling around Europe and staying in a "hostile," but what should be said are words like ridiculous, dumb, provincial, and downright dirty. If the goal is to meet Europeans and learn the culture, note that generally a "hostile" is only full of other Americans who read the more conventional travel guides. When deciding on a place for lodging in Paris, or anywhere in Europe, always begin with the question, "Would I do this in the United States?" In fact, that mantra is a good one to adopt when making any decision involving world travel. When visiting New York or Los Angeles or Atlanta, the first instinct is never to ask, "Where are the good hostels?" Therefore, it shouldn't be adopted in Paris. There are too many horror stories about robbery and sexual crimes, along with poor conditions of "hostiles" for anyone to ever consider utilizing their services. Also, don't count on the convenience of a hot shower to wash away any of the general griminess, either.

Hotels

Anything short of renting an apartment at the Ritz might be a disappointment, but *Beyond Your Means* travelers know that saving money on lodging means you can be all the more extravagant in other escapades. But keep in mind the extreme comfort costs of staying at hotels, which might be easily within your means. Always ask the question, "What good is saving a little 'geld' if my room has the same general comfort and temperature as a mud hut in East Africa? " Therefore, the *Beyond Your Means* black-letter law is to stay at a low-priced three-star hotels during the summer and possibly at a two-star during the other months. Taking the risk of staying at a two-star hotel during the summer is at your own peril, and we cannot be held responsible for the fact that you will be bathing in pools of your own sweat due to the lack of air conditioning.

Three-star hotels always have air conditioning, and when the abject cruelty of the summer inflicts its wrath on Paris, you better pray that you've secured the appropriate lodging ahead of time. Although not suggested, the rules can be bent if you can find lesser accommodations that have your optimal climate conditions. Go ahead and stay there, but don't expect a round-the-clock effort by the maintenance staff if your A/C unit happens to go offline for a bit. If cash is running low and the credit card companies aren't being flexible, remember that Accor is a French company, and while Tom Bodett may not leave the light on for you, Pierre will be happy to give you a *chambre* for a night at a reasonable price.

Another thing most Parisian hotels have, with *Beyond Your Means* travelers in mind, is business cards at their front desks with a small map on the back, clearly identifying your hotel in regards to the surrounding area. Make sure to take at least one with you before you leave for the evening. Cab drivers in Paris are renowned for pretending not to understand pidgin French. They are particularly uninterested in deciphering slurred pidgin French and—God forbid—you try it in English. Therefore, a hotel card handed to a cab driver can make the journey back to bed easier and a lot less circumstantial.

Long-Term

The social cachet and cultural reasons for staying as long as possible have been discussed previously but are worthy of a second mention. Countless times in a *Beyond Your Means* traveler's life, friends and family may criticize certain decisions that are made, which generally lack responsibility. Just think, however, of the great satisfaction that comes with knowing that those same individuals back home will eventually be asked about your whereabouts, and they will have to answer "living in Paris." The longer your trip, the more likely it will be that they will have to utter those words, while logging their hours in the accounting department, worrying about their 401(k).

Finding an apartment for the longer-term traveler is more than worth it. Having an apartment not only makes you feel like you are living in Paris but will certainly prove useful on those nights that aren't spent alone. Additionally, remain cognizant of the fact that if the apartment is furnished, it will definitely have most of the amenities of a home.

Other than the social currency of having your own place, an apartment can actually become a lighter tax on resources. If traveling during the summer, finding a relatively inexpensive apartment is no problem, as many Parisians spend extended holidays outside of the city. The best way to locate a *pied-à-terre* is to start at a broker's office in the neighborhood where you want to live. As long as you have a couple of days to waste looking at apartments, this is the superior solution. If time is of the essence or you just want a place to call home as soon as you land, then reserving through the Internet works as well. Be advised, though, that staying in someone else's apartment is usually going to come with a hefty upfront deposit, as well as a broker finder's fee. As long as you're not going to Paris as a roadie for the Rolling Stones, you should expect to get the money back.

While renting an apartment is highly recommended, a discerning word on Parisian apartments is in order. Paris is a very old city and it does not, in most respects, knock down its old apartment structures to build new ones. Napoleon III did an excellent job of remodeling the city, but unfortunately, that was one of the last major upgrades that many of the older buildings received. What you get for an apartment in Paris might be surprising. Air ventilation can be atrocious, plumbing can turn on you like a slighted mythological god, and kitchens might appear archaic. Paramount to all of this is that there is little, if any, privacy in Paris. Most apartments are built right on top of one another, with walls about as substantial as a sorority girl in a sumo wrestling match. Coupled with this is the fact that many Parisian apartment complexes are built with a hollow, gardenless courtyard in the middle, which acts like a megaphone for sound coming out of the apartments. Chanting a rousing rendition of *Allez les Bleu,* or "go-fight-win," out your window like a cheerleader at a pep rally is interesting at first blush, but any extracurricular noises made after dark will also have the same amplification. The point is that even if you are being quiet, someone else probably thinks you are not.

Places to look for apartments in Paris:

- www.craigslist.com

- www.nyhabitat.com

- www.parisattitude.com

- www.apartment-paris.com

- www.parishome.com

- www.fusac.fr

Additionally, real estate agencies, or *Agences de Location*, appear in the Yellow Pages under *Agences de Location d'appartements et de propriétés* and *Location d'appartements*. If you are willing to spend time locating just the right place, below are a few real estate agencies with English-speaking staff:

Century 21, France S.A., Bat D
3 rue des Cévennes, Petite
Montagne Sud,
CE 1701
91017 Evry Cedex Lisses
Tel: 01 69 11 12 21
Web site: www.century21france.fr

Expat Prestige Service
8 rue Gounod
92210 Saint-Cloud
Tel: 01 46 02 23 83
E-mail: eps.1@wanadoo.fr

Flatotel
14, rue du Théâtre
75015 Paris
Tel: 01 45 75 62 20
Web site: www.locaflat.com

Les Citadines
120 Jean-Jaurès, Levallois Paris
Cedex 92532
Tel: 0 825 010 343
Web site: www.citadines.com
E-mail: societes@citadines.com

For quite a different cultural experience during a long-term stay, investigate the possibility of living with native Parisians. It is not uncommon for roommates to sublet a room in their apartment to travelers, simply to have a cultural experience themselves. These individuals will prove invaluable in locating excellent *bistros* and nightspots. In the same vein, renting a room from a French family can provide an unmatched opportunity for cultural immersion. Many families will include meals and cleaning services in the price of rent and may be interested in having a foreigner around for the enlightening experience as well; thus, they can serve as guides for the city.

The same perils, however, exist in Paris as with roommates domestically. An additional concern with renting from a family is that there may be children in the household; thus, it may not be appropriate to bring "friends" home for the evening or to enter the house after a certain time. Moreover, sometimes the parents will want a boarder to engage in lots of discourse with them for the intellectual stimulation. If this is your cup of tea, then by all means consider this possibility. But a word to the wise: avoid the topic of politics at all costs.

Le meilleur ami de l'homme

After scouring the Internet for hours, looking for an apartment to meet my very specific standards, it became clear that in order to find the perfect location, I would need to spend a few days wandering around the neighborhood where I wanted to live. Being the type who instantly needs to unpack, however, and pretend that wherever my proverbial hat is hanging is home, this approach simply wouldn't do, leading me to consider an alternative. While perusing the Internet for an apartment, I ran across several ads from French families interested in having a young foreigner live with them for the summer. After contacting one of the ad-posters, I thought about the wonderful opportunities I would have to improve my French and observe a functioning French family in their native habitat. While this hadn't been my first choice for lodging, I was very excited about the opportunity.

When I arrived in Paris and entered my new home, I instantly began learning the advantages and disadvantages of this arrangement. It became blatantly clear that I had forgotten to ask how high the ceiling was in what would be my bedroom. Since the room was a converted attic, my style was, quite literally, cramped. The family, however, seemed nice, and there was no reason to complain at that late in the juncture. They were already a bit surprised by my very American-style packing habits; thus, there was no reason to trouble them further. Besides the ceiling height, the biggest drawback was the very large, very imposing family dog. This proud shepherd, named "Indio," was a great dog but a terrible housemate. Being loyal and protective, he would bark and growl at my every move. At nights, when entering the house at 4:00 a.m., Indio made sure that the entire house was aware of my rather late arrivals. "Indio, arrêt!" became as common of a greeting to me as "bonjour" did during the day. In getting to know the family, however, I found myself immersed in a part of Paris that I never expected.

The husband and wife were an interesting duo—the wife an advisor to the European Union, and the husband, a rock musician. Photos of both their lives proudly decked the halls of the rather spacious house in the 13th arrondisement. The husband was hard at work on a new style of music, Brazilian-French fusion. During my entire stay, I never quite understood which part of the music was Brazilian and which part was French, but it was certainly enjoyable and led to many invitations for me to attend small concerts around Paris. The house was full of activity, with musicians coming and going at all hours and well-dressed political-types having lunch there on a daily basis.

The restrictions that came with living in a house with others while I was staying out all night were a bit much at times, but the experience as a whole is something I would never trade and certainly encourage others to try, at least once.

How to Finance Your Trip: Consulting Your Patrons

Beyond Your Means travelers are, at their very cores, artists. Well, maybe they own some art. At the very least they've seen art on a wall somewhere and may feel that their opinions of it are as good as any famed critic. The dilemma for these travelers is that they love to live life more extravagantly than their resources allow. Consequently, much like a Roman poet, they must secure patronage from others. While the patrons of yesteryear went by such names as Gaius Maecenas and <u>Medici</u>, today they go by monikers like Visa, MasterCard, and the federal government.

Credit Cards

The use of credit cards can be deployed in two separate instances: first, booking a flight to Paris, and second, paying for your activities while there.

Any true credit-card junkie has at least thought how great his life as a world traveler would be if he obtained a credit card that allowed him to earn valuable miles for his purchases. This concept is brought to you by the same advertisement agency that gave us the Pet Rock. The grim reality is that you always end up paying more through the interest rates than it would actually cost to buy your ticket outright anyway. Because it seems like free money, many people keep going back to the whipping post, year after year, which only perpetuates those pieces of plastic poison. Therefore, it should come as no surprise that these remain unendorsed as a consumer good by the *Beyond Your Means* Travel Association. The only redeeming quality for these cards comes in the unlikely event that the minimum balance is always paid, but that still doesn't mitigate the high interest rate. Considering that all too frequently, your credit card may serve as the tab for an entire friend group, you could have more frequent flyer miles than a foreign diplomat, but instead of traveling for free, you pay for each and every mile you earn—sometimes twice.

One the other hand, do not confuse the lack of endorsement for frequent-flyer-mile credit cards as a dismissal of all credit cards. Quite to the contrary, what we do endorse are frivolous and extemporaneous spending habits, which means reliance on credit cards as a foundation for a lifestyle. Utilizing these wallet-sized friends to their fullest potential takes great planning. If, for instance, spending a lot of cash over a long period of time is the goal, it is recommended that you keep up-to-date on at least the minimum balance for six months to a year. This is usually the period of time it will take for a credit card company to tattoo you with the "good credit" phraseology. This mark-of-the-beast label means you'll most likely be granted the credit increase you requested before you can safely "max plastic" in Paris.

Another trick many *Beyond Your Means* travelers aren't above resorting to are half-truth answers in response to questions about annual income. This works best when obtaining a new credit card, rather than getting an increase on an existing one. Remember, it is household income that the credit card companies want to know about. Since some *Beyond Your Means* travelers aren't ever financially emancipated from their parents, it is acceptable to include the parents' annual incomes into the household war chest that the evil purveyors of plastic want to know about. Perhaps if your current living situation includes several roommates, including their income and their family incomes as well might be exactly what is needed to establish the initial credit line you deserve.

The half-truth philosophy may be extended to your current occupation, depending on the particular company, in which case it may be difficult to say that a new public school teacher brings home a half-million per year. If asked about your current occupation, the half-truth philosophy likely transforms to the whole-lie approach. Therefore, employing creative linguistics will win the day. Certain professions will never be questioned, despite the actual stated income. For example, after stating a date of birth that calculates to an age somewhere in the mid-20s, simply offer that you are a "surgeon" or "lawyer." While it is impossible for a completely inflated income to be justified by either of these glorified professions, any questioning will likely dissipate. It is never too off base to claim a profession that is related to your own. A drug-store clerk can become a pharmaceutical representative almost as fast as someone who is unemployed can become a consultant or writer. Also, using the impressive occupations of friends and relatives may be a useful strategy.

Student Loans

College students are intimately familiar with the process of securing federal financing for their summer vacations by masking them as study-abroad programs. Funding a Parisian pleasure trip, however, is not just limited to those earning degrees. Under the guise of education, savvy *Beyond Your Means* travelers can maximize their ability to spend what they don't have at the very lowest interest rates in exchange for the most minimal of academic efforts.

The facts are as follows: If you are going to be studying in Paris in any program that is affiliated with a U.S.-accredited institution by the Department of Education, then you're eligible for federal funding. The Department of

Education will also give its blessing to a handful of higher-learning institutions outside of the U.S., so check to see if an exception applies. Private language schools, whose principal place of business is actually in the U.S., may also have a relationship with lenders; therefore, inquiring with the school itself about financial-aid options is the best policy.

There is also the option to shackle yourself with a private loan. These loans are basically personal loans in disguise, but are simply called "student loans" to make them appear more debtor-friendly. While you will have to pay a much higher interest rate and possibly need a co-signer, depending on credit history, to secure this type of funding, these loans do offer payment deferment options and lower interests than a credit card. Moreover, the interest on student loans can often be tax deductible, depending on the loan type, and in general, a multi-year forbearance is rather easy to secure. At the very least, student loans should be considered an option over the Plastic Shylocks. Consult the following for such a loan:

Non-degree seeking:

Citibank: 800-967-2400, CitiAssist Loan, www.studentloan.citibank. com

U.S. Bank: 800-242-1200, No Fee Education Loan, www.usbank.com/ nofeeapp

U.S. Bank: 800-242-1200, Gap Education Loan, www.usbank.com/ gapapp

Parents

Of course, many *Beyond Your Means* travelers are never fully independent from what seems like a bottomless financial source: parents. A number of readers may be at a point in life where parental funding is no longer necessary, but for those who aren't, never hesitate to try and gain their pecuniary support. *Beyond Your Means* travelers are well-rounded and have such valuable skills as speaking Swedish, but the reality is that immediate family members often lost faith in their gaining independence years ago. Needless to say, despite their increasing thinly veiled insults, parents have most likely accepted the reality of having a *Beyond Your Means* child. Often, the relationship that readers have with their parents has diminished greatly, due to phone calls regarding the damning monthly credit-cards bills, leading to silence from fathers and concern from mothers. Therefore, securing parental funding for at least part of the vacation to Paris requires strategic planning. There's an art to winning over dear old Dad, and it comes in the form of the "PR visit home." Think of it as a presidential candidate who neglects his home state and must make a last-ditch effort home to ensure victory. The formula is simple: the voters at home love the candidate and just need to be reminded that he loves them, too.

Penny-Pinching and Saving

This works, too.

What to Bring

The trip has been rationalized and financed, companions have been selected, so now the only thing left to do is decide what to take with you—and why. By no means is this a lighthearted decision, but following some simple etiquette will guide you in the right direction.

A rather simple ensemble can either be enhanced or derogated by accessories. Currently, at least in the United States, the fashion and accessories that are all the rage were previously only acceptable at a Monster Truck rally. Some Americans think that sporting a plastic mesh trucker's hat is more sartorially elegant than, say, a man scarf. Note that it isn't really clear how or why truck drivers became the twenty-first century's Cary Grant.

The classic rule in travel is to pack appropriately for what you plan to be doing. If you're going to be camping and hiking through the mountains, then trainers, T-shirts, and cargo pants are acceptable. Chances are, if you're traveling to Paris, there will be no need for camping gear at a bistro or museum. And just to be clear, no one considers Montmartre an actual mountain or faraway encampment anymore. Odds are the only hiking you will be doing is up the steps to *Sacré-Cœur*, but most *Beyond Your Means* travelers will opt for the tram ride up instead or avoid this tourist trap altogether.

Despite the notorious assumptions regarding Parisians and how rude they can be, Paris isn't all that dissimilar to cities elsewhere. Expect to be treated according to how you present yourself. In essence, if you go somewhere dressed like a vagabond, expect to be regarded as one. You wouldn't go out in your closest metropolitan city for dinner dressed for a NASCAR race, so why would such dress be acceptable in a city renowned for high-end everything? While the thesis that the French aren't any more pretentious than other cultures has yet to gain academic acceptance, it still holds that the idea itself isn't all that far-fetched.

Your Social Success through Dress

It is not yet clear where the myth started that the rigors of travel excuse the burdens of an acceptable personal appearance. The correct premise is that there is no license to ignore a germane dress code merely because you are outside your comfortable homeland. Sage advice that a *Beyond Your Means* traveler references daily is borrowed from the English: "A gentleman always wears a collar." To decrease the chances of ever being completely out of place, always keep a collared shirt on the ready.

In general, Europeans tend toward a much smarter and more sophisticated style, and the French often hold advanced degrees in this discipline. But bear in mind that they have been crafting their cultural appearance for generations. Transitioning from your home culture, where most anything is acceptable, to a locale where citizens pride themselves on being slaves to fashion is often tricky for those unfamiliar with our well-heeled advice. Therefore, emulation is not recommended. In particular, it is difficult for the modern North American male to formulate a convincingly French look; consequently, the current *Beyond Your Means* think-tank position is to try and look more British. Trust us; it's easier to throw together a pair of light trousers, a cutaway collar shirt, and austere cuff links than to pull off a runway collection. There is no fooling the French, or anyone else, when an American who is used to wearing tennis shoes with khakis to a cubicle every day decides to don skin-tight pants and a pink scarf. Anything, however, would essentially be an improvement over wearing a Phish T-shirt and Adidas snap pants.

For Gentlemen …

After careful reflection, the following is the official *Beyond Your Means* position on dress for gentlemen: In the summer, a collared polo shirt or light cotton shirt with khaki pants or shorts should be worn, with an eye on the daily temperature. For the fall, gentlemen should consider adding a light sports coat, trousers, and a collared button-down shirt. The winter calls for a slightly weightier wardrobe—at the very least, a jacket at dinner. Sweaters are also a possibility, depending on the chill in the air. Remember, though, Paris is a café city, and Parisians are willing to eat outside, regardless of the time of year or the temperature. Blankets and heat lamps are quite common as buffers against the cold. To a *Beyond Your Means* traveler, spring is basically the same season as fall, only with brighter colors; therefore, make the necessary adjustments and keep classic.

... and the Dames

For women, a few carefully selected pieces will suffice, at least through the *"Bonjour. Je m'appelle ___"* part of the conversation. First, black is your friend. You don't need to incorporate it sparingly, although the all-black look is best left to those who have perfected it elsewhere, unless the goal is to look like a fan of The Smiths. But basic-black pants go with everything, everywhere, and can easily be brightened up with a splash of color, so pack more than one pair.

All women need to pay close attention to the rules regarding scarves. It is imperative to leave behind that knitted number with the pom-poms adorning the end, and opt for a real scarf. Buy it there—it doesn't have to be Hermès (although, of course …). One caveat: there is a technique to scarf-wearing that American women are generally not privy to. Although they were briefly *en vogue* a couple of decades ago to balance the masculinity of shoulder pads, scarves have somewhat receded from the American fashion landscape, largely because few women feel they know how to wear them properly. Look for guidance from French women, or ask a salesperson at *Le Printemps* to show you. If you simply cannot master the scarf discipline, a pashmina can always be a great substitute in a pinch. Plus, it is good for slightly chilly cafés.

And of course, there is always the famous little black dress. There's a reason it was developed in France. Enough said.

For Everyone

After great deliberation, especially concerning the obvious implications internationally, the official *Beyond Your Means* philosophy concerning jeans and shoes has been formulated. Jeans are now acceptable in almost all social situations, but some amount of personal discretion will be necessary. For example, jeans at a casual dinner are fine, but jeans during a private dinner cruise on the Seine won't be appropriate. A cardinal rule involving jeans, however, is that no matter when worn, they should never be ostentatiously adorned with painted designs, studs, or multiple zippers. Painter jeans shouldn't really be in your wardrobe, anyway, so don't bring them to Paris.

Shoes are often the dead giveaway of an out-of-towner. Because shoes are heavy and take up a lot of room, the unsophisticated have incorrectly continued to argue that less is more. It is suggested that you bring along any or all shoes that could possibly be utilized. Don't be afraid to include more formal shoes in your bag if you think you will need them *de temps en temps*. For women, forget all that nonsense about comfort. (Women who aren't willing to sacrifice comfort for style likely didn't read past the introduction anyway.) High-heeled boots are a must, but a warning: cobblestones are poison for heels. They may be ruined, but you will look fabulous in the process.

Male *Beyond Your Means* travelers, however, are expected to follow the minimal rule that you can at least take a loafer home to meet your parents. Leather-soled loafers are the perfect go-between. Loafers also suggest a more relaxed, intellectual look that all true *Beyond Your Means* travelers strive for. Our arch nemesis, Rick Steves, prefers white sneakers at dinner or other footwear, the most redeeming quality of which is "a good tread." Leave the treads to Goodyear. As a general rule, avoid anything recommended by Rick that is also the standard in many Silicon Valley cubicles. Despite what he thinks, people don't exactly want to eat with Rick, because he's dressed to walk the track rather than to enjoy a three-course meal. We'd tell you to choose wisely, but we know you already have.

It is also recommended to have the appropriate accessories and fashions for the image you want to portray. There are many popular images for a foreigner traveling in Paris. While these travelers do not necessarily socialize with one another, they still are all members of the same *Beyond Your Means* family. All know the image they want to project to the rest of the world, whether it is true or not. If it is the Hemingway-esque American writer type you want locals and tourists to take you for, then develop a wardrobe that includes a bush shirt, plenty of khakis, and possibly a bulky roll-neck sweater. Maybe it's the jet-setter look you want people to see; then, the rule is simple: all black. Always. An acceptable deviation is to possibly include one randomly placed piece of color, like a pink pocket square. A third popular image is English Public School or American Country Club Casual. This voyager needs to have plenty of popped collar shirts on hand, brown loafers, and plain-front trousers.

What Not to Bring (Possibly Not Even Own)

It is a familiar sight: American tourists wearing white sneakers, calf-high athletic socks, gym shorts without pockets, inappropriate T-shirts, and X-Men-style Oakley sunglasses. Knowing what not to take is possibly more important than knowing what to bring along. Major mistakes can be avoided, if certain negative enablers are not within reach. This basically means ignoring anything that is suggested by the backpacking demographic. Remember, these are the folks seen blundering through the streets, carrying everything they "need" for their trip. A *Beyond Your Means* traveler doesn't attach his shoes and Nalgene trail bottle to whatever receptacle is housing his belongings for the summer. Therefore, when packing for Paris, view with great skepticism anything suggested by the backpacking set in terms of clothing—or, as a matter of fact, anything else.

Since so much has been written by and for backpackers, understanding the backpacker mentality is a great starting point when thinking of what *not* to bring on a trip to Paris. Again, there is something to be said for traveling around Europe with everything you'll use on your back. Thousands of years ago, nomadic hunters used to do the same thing, but they did it for survival. Here in the twenty-first century, such travel is no longer necessary. God bless progress. There are two types of backpackers: the paleo-packer and the neo-packer. The male paleo-packer is generally unshaven, wears lots of earth tones, bathes weekly, wears hiking boots everywhere, is never without a copy of Gandhi's biography, and advocates French socialism for the United States. Together, he and his female counterpart attempt to let everyone they meet at the hostel know of their depth, despite having been raised in Orlando and Evanston, respectively.

The neo-packer is a little easier to spot as a uniquely American invention. The male neo-packer wears Adidas pants and New Balance tennis shoes and thinks he knows how to play the guitar. His female counterpart wears the same attire and interned once for the ACLU. The neo-packers often take a trip down the Champs-Élysées or Avenue Montaigne and have no qualms about walking into Christian Dior or Chanel wearing cargo shorts and then complaining about the rude French clerks who wouldn't assist them. Both paleo- and neo-packers have a respect for one another and often exchange pleasantries at the local Starbucks, if it serves Fair Trade coffee. The backpacker mentality has infiltrated so much of travel culture that it provides endless amounts of amusement for *Beyond Your Means* travelers.

Proper dress is something that too many Americans resist. A walk through some of the more popular areas for American tourists—for instance, the 5th or 6th arrondissement—can offer the most tragic and comedic displays of appearance. Some of the favorites the *Beyond Your Means* thinkers have encountered over the years include:

- **Lumberjack apparel.** This would be great if you were going on a moose-sighting tour in Norway, but you're actually touring the Louvre that day. Leave the flannel shirt and hiking boots at home.

- **Pants with zip-off legs**. This again comes to us from our favorite adversary, Rick Steves. You're not going fishing. If these must be an accompaniment because you've decided they are extremely versatile and convenient, perhaps also consider packing a fishing hat with the lures fashionably stuck into it. Plenty of camouflage will also be useful. You'll be sure to remain completely inconspicuous while dressed like the proprietor of a Bait & Tackle shop during a tour of Versailles. Just because a fashion icon like Marie Antoinette was deposed there doesn't mean her memory should be trampled upon.

- **T-shirts with obnoxious slogans on them**. Nothing says cool quite like advertising your supposed epic manhood with a "Big Johnson" tee. After all, any erudite Frenchman couldn't help but be impressed by the slogan "Liquor up front. Poker in the rear." Faux Jack Daniel's/Absolut Vodka T-shirts advertising a party you went to should also be left at home, preferably in a dumpster. Also, while fraternity and sorority shirts from the best houses at Iowa State and LSU may have credibility on campus, they seem to lack something in Oberkampf. The list can go on and on. The idea, though, is not to overuse T-shirts in Paris and to limit them to trips to the gym.

- **Fanny packs.** These are recommended by virtually all travel guides, and because they stand for everything we stand against, fanny packs should be considered anathema to all *accoutrements*. The majority of people who can be seen sporting these tourist advertisements are also the ones wearing elastic-band gym shorts. It simply must be that no one has ever informed them that trousers with pockets have been on the market for quite some time. *Beyond Your Means* travelers rarely, if ever, need to resort to additional storage capacity when gallivanting through the streets of Paris. If this becomes necessary, a messenger bag is recommended, which should adequately release you from the social stigma and confines associated with the fanny pack.

- **Bulky cameras.** In the era of modern technology, small digital cameras have become the norm, but it is still common to see tourists in Paris walking about with monstrosities from a previous generation dangling from their belts. The advice on this point is to leap past the Polaroid 1980s and upgrade to something more manageable and less embarrassing.

- **Jean shorts**. Nothing more needs to be said.

Also falling in the leave-at-home category are toiletries. For some reason, certain sects of society are under the mistaken belief that essentially the same items are not sold in metropolitan France as in, say, Omaha, Nebraska. However, they are. Therefore, packing that bottle of shampoo or extra deodorant is not necessary. Remember that the commercials that tout "L'Oreal: Paris" aren't an international conspiracy. Superfluous toiletries only take up more room in your suitcase that could otherwise be devoted to more necessary things, like an extra pair of shoes. Besides, *Beyond Your Means* travelers would much rather use French toiletries than Pert Plus while abroad

Things to Do Before Departing

While it may be contrary to a *Beyond Your Means* traveler's very core belief system, some form of pre-planning is necessary in order to have a successful venture to France. Generally, those reading this guide have been too busy promoting their trip to ponder important details surrounding it. Even though all of your friends are already well aware of your impending departure date, there are still a few highly important issues that should be handled before leaving. For example, it is best to resolve questions beforehand about access to funds and what to do if you become ill while in France. Since *Beyond Your Means* travelers aren't normally bothered with trivial things and are more apt to use their time to drop references regarding their worldliness, many should consult the following information before boarding the plane:

Banking

Some travel guides will recommend changing all money into euros or travelers checks before departing from home and keeping it in a secure location. This just doesn't make sense. In the continuing theme of reminding readers that Europeans use all modern conveniences, don't be afraid to use an ATM (CashPoints) in Paris. Just like in the good ol' USA, when running low on cash and needing a Big Gulp, there are ATMs around every corner.

Be leery of ATMs only for the fact that there may be high fees charged by your bank at home for using them, in addition to the fee charged by the ATM company. Ultimately, these fees will not be markedly higher than the fees charged at an exchange service, as long as you withdraw a respectable amount of scratch.

There are several ways to avoid these fees altogether. The first recommended way is to find the Paris locations of your American bank. It would be a miracle if the First National Bank of Branson had a branch to handle foreign withdrawals, but many American banks are rather far-reaching and have offices abroad. For example, consider these options:

Chase Bank
14, Place Vendôme
75001 Paris
Tel: 01 40 15 45 00

Citibank
125 Ave des Champs-Élysée
75008 Paris
Tel: +33.53.23.33.60

Another recommendation is to check with your bank to see if there is a reciprocity agreement that provides for non-fee withdrawals. These agreements are common and worth a call before departure or searching for the information after making frequent trips to French ATMs. Furthermore, having an account with a truly international bank that has numerous ATMs throughout Paris will prove invaluable. For instance, HBSC is a tried-and-true friend of many *Beyond Your Means* adventurers because of their broad reach and non-fee withdrawals worldwide. Your specific financial plan needs to be arranged ahead of time, so your entire life savings is readily accessible at any given point.

A *Beyond Your Means* Traveler's Best Friend: American Express

American Express offers several services that a *Beyond Your Means* traveler may want to utilize, even if only to feel important and add to a self-constructed image. The first is mail service. Since the advent of e-mail, using "snail mail" may seem a bit passé, but there will be times when it is still necessary. For example, if your journey began by leaving your boss a voicemail saying you would be gone for a month, it may be your former employer's policy to send a hard copy of termination notices. American Express offers mail services to their customers for just such occasions.

The policy is that mail/letters, not packages, can be sent to a participating American Express location for pickup by an American Express customer. It must be picked up within thirty days. The best part is that there is no charge for this service, but the specifics of the policy should be clarified with individual offices. Even if you aren't expecting a termination notice, there is nothing more gratifying than receiving mail in a foreign country—and it gives the feeling of yesteryear.

Additionally, American Express offers services on foreign currency. Customers can purchase a variety of foreign currencies at participating American Express locations. American Express advises that it is best to call prior to arrival to arrange the currency of choice, as some currencies may need to be ordered. If calling is too inconvenient, however, it is a good bet that in France, the euro will be readily available. Note that service fees may apply and turn-around time for receipt can vary by location. The central American Express office in Paris is located at:

American Express Foreign Exchange Services
11 Rue Scribe
75009 Paris
Tel: +33.47.77.79.28

Hospitals

Identifying the location of an English-speaking hospital is a burdensome but necessary step for all travelers, not just those traveling *Beyond Your Means* and not because the water quality is of any concern in Western Europe. There may be instances when illness, either self-induced or otherwise, requires a trip to *l'hôpital* to see *un médecin*. When complaining about aches and pains, it is likely better for all involved to speak in English, so take note of these hospitals with a large English-speaking staff:

American Hospital
63 bd. Victor Hugo
92202 Neuilly sur Seine
Tel: +33.46.41.25.25

Hertford British Hospital
3 rue Barbes
92300 Levallois-Perret
Tel: +33.46.39.22.22

Hospital Foch
40 rue Worth
92150 Suresnes
Tel: +33.46.25.20.00

Keep in mind that in many European countries, France included, you can go to an apothecary for basic medical and first-aid care—just look for the sign with the green cross. Many more things are sold over-the-counter there, and the pharmacists are often bilingual and very helpful.

Driving

There may come a time when instead of choosing to venture out of the city via plane or train, you'll choose to travel by automobile. The first thought that comes to mind is that your state-issued driver's license may have no standing in France. It would be nonsensical to think that the state of South Dakota's judgment on driving ability would influence a sovereign nation. That seemingly odd logic, however, does apply. A temporary visitor to France—that is, someone who is there for fewer than ninety days—may use a valid driver's license issued in the United States. Clearly, this is one of the few instances when France will readily give deference to the legal decisions made in Austin.

Visitors are, however, encouraged to have an international driving permit. Securing this before leaving the United States is fairly easy. This document is valid for one year and is attainable from any domestic American Automobile Association (AAA) office. The cost is somewhere between $10 and $20, depending on your membership status with the all-powerful automobile lobby. The international driving permit is not necessary unless you are involved in an accident or cited for traffic violations, a strong possibility for a *Beyond Your Means* traveler who chooses to drive.

Luggage

At the outset of the trip, you may have lofty goals and expectations of not spending all the money to which you have access. But once the dream slowly fades to a distant memory, and the luggage seems too heavy and cumbersome, consider shipping certain items home before departing. After all, by the end of a trip, *Beyond Your Means* travelers will be looking for a way to needlessly spend their few remaining cash reserves. Consider using the Paris-based company *Setavion*, which specializes in the shipment of unaccompanied air baggage. They can be contacted at:

Rue des 2 cèdres, Bat. 5 Zone de Fret 3
95707 Roissy Charles de Gaulle
Tel: +33.48.62.33.47

A piece of advice to heed is to never have so much luggage that the need for shipping anything is necessary. But many *Beyond Your Means* travelers refuse to abide by conventional wisdom, so checking with FedEx or UPS is another option. These services may even prove more realistic and more "within your means" than those that specialize in luggage transportation.

That being said, there are several business that specialize in luggage shipment around the world, from door to door. From a business perspective, luggage services are a terrible investment, as they have never been known for being highly profitable or lasting very long. But as a traveler who scoffs at the idea of being constricted or strained by the weight of luggage, alas, they are worthy of consideration.

Beyond Your Means travelers often deceive themselves into thinking that this particular trip will be the one where the bank isn't broken. Consequently, most elect to handle the luggage themselves. However, there is at least one perk about Charles de Gaulle Airport (CDG) and many European airports: the luggage carts, or "*chariots*," as the French so eloquently say, are generally free. On the downside, in the post-September 11 world, luggage storage is difficult, as all lockers have been removed. But fear not, CDG still has a baggage-holding service in Terminal 1. Given the current security environment, the only constraint is that you have to be pretty specific about the time you'll return for your luggage.

Nature versus Nurture

At a certain age and in certain circumstances, everyone faces a decision with what to do with themselves. Many of my personal decisions kept landing me in cubicles and classrooms full of serious types, who readily dismissed the idea of gallivanting off to Europe on a whim. These surroundings made me consider altering my outlook on life and start taking the big-boy path. In the middle of one particularly serious situation—law school—I began planning more seriously for my future. It is amazing how attractive a young man becomes to the opposite sex when he has actually developed the elusive "plan." Therefore, I spent an arduous amount of time seeking out summer clerkships that could one day lead to gainful employment. This would, hopefully, force my friends to stop mocking me. However, instead of making such a jump into adulthood, my own natural inclination emerged victorious, and my decision on how to spend the summer became clear—to blow lots of cash for "one last" romp through my favorite city, Paris.

By applying Beyond Your Means advice to my own life, I identified a "professional development" program to mask the experience as mature, while arranging co-financing between the federal government and Visa. The only thing left to do was secure housing and hop on a plane.

On the plane itself, my first real adventure began. To my dismay, I was seated beside a middle-aged man who was overly concerned with making sure that I knew he "usually flies first class but it was sold out this time." Of course, I took this opportunity and ran with it. After allowing him to regale me with his troubles in trying to be re-seated with the privileged set, I decided it was time to adopt my chosen Beyond Your Means character for this trip, which I hadn't settled on prior to it. When he asked what I did for a living, my response was "I'm a writer." Despite not having published a word since being an ill-begotten music reporter for my college newspaper, I saw no problem with taking great poetic license. I knew this man, a college professor, was more likely to be reading the Chronicle of Higher Education than anything else, so I took my limited previous experience and ran with it. As far as he was concerned, I was headed to Paris to research an emerging movement in French music for my new column in Rolling Stone.It felt good to talk about how well I knew Jann Wenner and the other folks in the magazine business and, thanks to the lack of Internet access at 30,000 feet, he was none the wiser. Needless to say, this tale put a quick end to his proselytizing about the many times when he'd called the first-class section home.

Arriving in Paris was a welcome moment for more than just the obvious reasons. The fact that the airplane video machine had been broken certainly did not add to the hours upon hours spent traversing the Atlantic. After deplaning and walking through the peculiar example of 1960s style décor that is Charles de Gaulle [Airport], I made a cardinal mistake near customs that I urge all Beyond Your Means travelers to avoid. While having been relatively near the front of the plane, my bladder demanded attention and sent me to the salle de bains, instead of directly to the customs line. In that three-minute time period, what would have been a brief time awaiting my stamp turned in to an hour as the line grew ponderous in my absence.

Perhaps the only thing that kept me going was the thought of the private car I had reserved to escort me from CDG to my temporary home. Since it was the beginning of the trip and the credit cards still had enormous limits, I had no problem justifying a questionable fiduciary decision. The French are anything but anti-egalitarian; therefore, having a uniformed man standing with my name on a placard at the CDG gate gave me the credibility that only frivolous spending can. Watching the other travelers as they realized they could only use French credit cards in the RER automated ticket machines made every centime worth it.

http://www.parishuttle.com/

4

Upon Arrival: The Essentials

A trip for any length of time will require a certain understanding of how to meet basic needs in Paris. Cultural immersion is the ultimate goal, but gaining at least an elementary mastery of the French interpretation of life's fundamentals will contribute additional elements to any vacation.

Before the baguettes, crêpes, and eventual bills, it is necessary to arrive at your chosen lodging. There are several ways to enter Paris from the airport, with some ways more tickling to the fancies of *Beyond Your Means* travelers than others. Ultimately, you can decide which path to take, but always bear in mind that recommendations for *Beyond Your Means* travelers never acknowledge obtuse frugality as a factor in the process.

Entering the City

Typically, other travel guides will recommend the RER system, which truth be told, is a cheap and efficient alternative to more elaborate means of transportation. However, dragging luggage and yourself on a crowded train is seldom a good idea; besides, a taxi is much more appealing. Taxis from CDG will drop you off at your destination while saving time and adding to convenience.

RER Info

The rapid RER train service links CDG with central Paris. Trains run every fifteen minutes (every eight minutes, in peak periods) and the journey takes approximately thirty-five minutes. Line B runs from the TGV station at

Terminal 2 to Gare du Nord, Châtelet-les-Halles, Saint-Michel, and Denfert-Rochereau, with connections to the métro.

Some *Beyond Your Means* travelers can't be bothered to take what seems like a longer and more arduous trip, so they opt for a taxi instead. The irony is that, depending on the time of day, the line for a cab could take much longer than actually carrying your bags to the RER station. Do also keep in mind two very important details: The particular motorized carriage one receives is a crapshoot, just same as anywhere else. And metropolitan Paris has a morning and afternoon rush hour as well. Many travelers end up rationalizing poor strategic decisions by concluding that at least their bags are safe in the trunk of the car, and they don't have to keep watch over them.

Transportation around the City

Keeping static rules about methods you'll use to travel around Paris can be great during conversations in which you want to appear like a man of the people or an entitled near-member of the peerage system, but they are not necessarily the best in practice. Hard and fast rules can result in long and expensive methods of transport, if one is not careful enough to weigh the appropriate factors.

Contrary to popular belief, taxis can be much more efficient and cost-effective than the métro. Taxis often make more sense than the métro if your journey time is short, and you have at least three people traveling along with you. Things that always need to be taken into account are outside temperature, distance to travel, time of day you'll be traveling, and exactly how much it would cost to ride underground.

An example of this is as follows: a hypothetical Ricknick accompanied by three other friends descend into a métro station in the middle of July at 8:00 p.m. to go from Ódean to Opéra for a fancy dinner. The four friends, after several transfers, finally reach their destination, only to trudge up the stairs and, with heavy perspiration on their brows and shirts, arrive at the restaurant (wearing sneakers, one would assume). The maître d' casts them to the side, as they appear to be quite an embarrassment in their current state. After around twenty-five minutes, they are invited to sit down at a table, which is far off into the corner of the restaurant, where few will have to endure the eyesore that the maître d' has decided they are. All told, the Ricknicks spent around €8 on their trip, had to wait an unreasonable period of time for a reservation, and were treated like social pariah when they arrived.

Contrast this with the fluid *Beyond Your Means* traveler going to the exact same place under the same conditions. This traveler knows that a taxi is more expensive than the métro, but he also knows that three friends are willing to split the cost. Taking a glance at a map, the *Beyond Your Means* traveler realizes that since Opéra isn't really that far from Ódean anyway, and since there are three other people with whom to split the bill, the best option is to consider the relative merits of a taxi. Traffic should remain light, considering the time of day, and the summer heat, if not managed, could result in the group looking less than presentable upon their arrival. Therefore, the *Beyond Your Means* posse goes to the taxi stand outside Ódean and pays €10 for a quick trip to the restaurant for their reservation. They also have to wait for their table, but only for five minutes, and they are offered complimentary *Kirs* as an aperitif for the inconvenience. They are seated at a table close to the window, with a view of the opera house across the street. The *Beyond Your Means* travelers spent €2 more than the Ricknicks, but the overall cost and result were worth it.

Unlike many other cities, taxis in Paris are loath to respond to your hailing them in the street. Paris has many dedicated taxi stands all over the city, where customers are expected to hire services. Parisians aren't accustomed to taxi-hailing aggressiveness and seem to find hailing a cab from the side of the road uncivilized. Interestingly enough, unshowered protesters dancing through tear-gas–filled streets six months a year is fine, but hailing a cab is actually quite coarse.

It logically follows that if there are instances where taking a taxi makes better overall sense than taking the métro, then the reverse is also true. On a crisp fall day, traveling by your lonesome during rush hour, the métro is surely your best option. Inflexibly refusing to take the métro because of social cachet or personal inconvenience is just bad policy, when you will have to spend ten times as much at triple the time to get to a specific destination in a taxi. Living *Beyond Your Means* is a great philosophy, but wasting money on transportation should be avoided. The Paris Métro is arguably the best on the planet. There are more stops going more places than any other métro system of comparable size. Although the métro learning curve is slightly steeper than the London Tube, and there is not air conditioning like the New York City Subway, it still has many conveniences that other cities don't. Be prepared to factor in the many variables that can give you the best possible outcome when choosing how to travel.

Another transportation point that is very difficult for Americans to understand is that taking the bus in Paris is not the mark of shame that it is in many other locales. It is a settled issue that no Atlanta debutante would be caught dead taking the express bus to Buckhead from the Piedmont Driving Club, but in Paris these rules aren't as stringent. The Paris bus system, much like its underground counterpart, is very efficient and among the world's best. Busses are air-conditioned and have routes that traverse the city in a way to maximize convenience. Also, some bus routes run all night, so if you plan to run out of cash on any particular evening, identifying the closest all-night bus route is highly advised.

Food

There are a couple of things you need to find right away when you arrive at your eventual destination in Paris, but the local McDonald's shouldn't be one of them. The temptation while at CDG may be to look for the American airport staple, Au Bon Pain, but keep in mind that France is the land that inspired this fast-food version of Parisian lifestyle. French food has been celebrated around the world for centuries, so take advantage of it. Just remember, despite the wonderful French restaurants in your hometown, odds are that the best place to eat French food is France. Comedians have noted that Americans do not always fully enjoy French food at home, since we are the culture that took the croissant and made it the croissanwich.

While it may be ideal to sample every five-star restaurant in town, enjoying small cafés and local *bistros* from time to time is the more sophisticated way to travel. Every neighborhood has a few stores you should be able to utilize at one time or another during your stay. Telling you to locate a café would be like telling you to find an establishment in Berlin that actually sells beer. Remaining in your neighborhood is much more enjoyable after your ex-pat routine has been determined. When rising in the morning, consider heading straight to the *boulangerie* (bakery) and pick up fresh croissants for breakfast before returning to your temporary home. The rest of the day can be spent loitering around the *tabac* or the various cafés your quarter offers.

Around lunchtime, you can eat up a good hour and a half going from the *crémerie* for cheese, to the *boucherie* (butcher) to pick up something meaty for lunch, and back to the *boulangerie* again for a warm baguette. Granted, one can do all of these things at the *supermarché* (supermarket) to save valuable time, but that's not really the *Beyond Your Means*—nor the Parisian—way.

By dinner time, you have the option to dine out or become the international gourmand that you claim to be. A lot of *supermarchés* have their own butcher and fishmonger section, the same as any super-store in your hometown. Therefore, you can easily go there to shop for everything at once. However, to dither for hours and obtain that truly authentic Parisian feeling, it is recommended that you buy each item individually at a specialty shop. Fish and other meats are purchased at the *poissonnerie* (fishmonger) or *boucherie*, respectively; vegetables at your local market; cheese at the *crémerie*; any desserts you might fancy at the *pâtisserie* (pastry shop); and anything else you might need at the *supermarché*. Of course, you can always head back to the *boulangerie* for any extra baguettes you require. The French rely on their bread like the Chinese depend upon rice. Thus, it's not uncommon for a Parisian to spend a tenth of his life at the baker's.

Another common problem *Beyond Your Means* travelers and inebriates alike face is where to eat after the restaurants and stores close. Unlike many cities, Parisians don't "run for the border" after hours. It seems their cultural refinement is too advanced to allow fast-food establishments to meet the demand of the consumer economy after 11:00 p.m. Therefore, it is highly recommended that *Beyond Your Means* travelers locate their nearest after-hours eatery. This will be an indispensable resource for those nights that turn into days. The following enterprises should be a good start:

- **Café le Départ St-Michel**, 1 place St-Michel (tel. **+33.43.54.24.55)**, Left Bank near St-Michel Métro, open twenty-four hours

- **Hippopotamus Restaurant & Grill,** various locations throughout Paris and France, open as late as 5:00 a.m. See their Web site for closest location: www.hippopotamus.fr/restaurant

Communication

Misconceptions in communication abound, especially while abroad. Nowadays it is assumed that all mobile phones work wherever you are—this isn't the case. Because not everyone took classes in the engineering quad, the reasons why are outside the scope of this discussion. All you need to know is if your current mobile carrier uses SIM technology. If they do, then you will be able to use your mobile in Paris. If they don't, then you'll be carting around a phone that has no prayer of working. The same rules apply in Paris as for any European country: without a SIM, you're not in. This concept, although quite elementary, has continued to cause confusion and frustration during travels aboard.

Receiving calls to your home mobile, however, may not be the most financially convenient way to go about things; neither is giving out your U.S. number to people you meet. Good *Beyond Your Means* travelers know this and plan accordingly. Instead of remaining dependant on their U.S. mobile, they bring along their own unlocked mobile. They then march into any mobile store and request the purchase of a SIM card. For around €40, and after about five minutes of *Pierre* pushing a bunch of buttons, *voila!* You now have a local French number and service. Doing it any other way is *très* uncool. You can also refill your minutes at the pivot point of French society, the *tabac*.

Lots of people wonder if bringing a computer has any merit whatsoever. Wi-Fi murdered the Internet café concept long ago, so if you're expecting to rely on one of those dinosaurs, *bonne chance*. Now, many cafés just happen to have Wi-Fi as well, so bringing your computer with you now makes good sense.

Tabacs

Tabacs are a source of everything, including food, coffee, cigarettes, alcohol, SIM cards, and just about anything else. Identifying the nearest one is among the first steps for your stay in Paris. It is odd to regular sensibilities to merge the café concept with convenience store and bar, but this is in line with the idea typically found in the South—the fusion of fried-chicken restaurant/gambling parlor/gas station/convenience store/tanning booth. *Tabacs* are essential to French society, so familiarizing yourself with them helps in a quick adjustment.

Keeping Clean

For the traveler staying in excess of one week, a dry cleaner could be very important. Again, this is something you'll find in virtually every neighborhood, but Parisian dry cleaners are notorious the world over for their lack of anything that could be described as diligence when trying to remove a stain or clean your clothes. Therefore, be advised; what might be routine for your garments at home is asking *l'impossible* in Paris. It is also not unheard of for a Paris dry cleaner to accept your clothes, charge you for their "work," and hand them back to you in the same condition as you brought them in. Your best bet is to find out who does the dry cleaning for an upscale hotel.

If nasty red-wine stains are commonplace for you, as they are for many *Beyond Your Means* travelers, then be advised that *Claude et la Madame* have their own products for stain-fighting. However, if you have access to a washing machine, you should be able to rectify any problems. While in the *supermarché*, be on the lookout for an ultra-small, scalene-triangle-shaped bottle. There are many different types of these products and each is specially formulated to combat specific elements, so you should be able to remove most stains (not just red wine) that you encounter.

But overall, having access to your own laundry facilities will add to your experience, as Parisian Laundromats are notoriously expensive. It is highly possible to spend €20 simply for a couple loads of your delicates. If you do not have access to your own facilities, then grin and bear the costs and plan to cram as much into one load as possible.

Rendez-vous **Points**

If traveling with companions, convenient *rendez-vous* points will be necessary. It is likely that at least the non-*Beyond Your Means* individual in the group won't have a working phone; thus, determining creative yet specific meeting places throughout the city will prove highly valuable. As a cardinal rule, while meeting at the Eiffel Tower may seem like a good idea, it will be all but impossible to locate your group in a sea of thousands of non-*Beyond Your Means* travelers, all anxiously awaiting the opportunity to fill their disposable cameras with images that are easily copied from the Internet. This is where creativity becomes an asset. Think about places that are a bit off the beaten path, yet so specific as to eliminate confusion. A possible idea would be the country music section at the Virgin Megastore on the Champs-Élysée. A Las

Vegas bookie would readily take the bet that this will be among the least-crowded parts of the entire city. Of course, tech-savvy *Beyond Your Means* travelers often utilize a GPS.

To ensure that no members of a group have a reason to miss an important event, such as annoying fellow bar patrons with impromptu and obnoxious singing, specific meeting places are essential.

Embassies

It is bound to happen at some point—be it a scenario where you are trying to impress others with the number of stamps you've received, or just casual disregard for something that has already served its initial purpose, passports run the risk of getting lost. While it may eventually be a potentially funny story, this situation must be rectified as soon as possible—so a trip to your respective embassy becomes inevitable. Take note of the location and procedure beforehand. The following destinations are quite used to weary travelers losing important documents:

United States Embassy
Office of American Services
2, rue Saint-Florentin
75001 Paris Cedex 08
Métro: Concorde

Embassy of Canada
Canadian Consular Service
35, avenue Montaigne
75008 Paris
Tel.: +33.44.43.29.02
Métro: Franklin D. Roosevelt

Australian Embassy
4 Rue Jean Rey
75724 Paris Cedex 15
Tel: +33.40.59.33.00
Métro: Bir-Hakeim or Champ de Mars-Tour Eiffel

New Zealand Embassy
7ter, rue Léonard de Vinci
75116 Paris
Tel: +33.45.01.43.43
Métro: Victor Hugo

Each embassy has a different routine, so before going it is best to inquire if there is a better time than others. For example, the American Embassy recommends going on a Thursday, as this is generally the least busy day. However, if the French decide that your visit coincides with the best time to begin another revolution, rest assured that there will not be an empty time slot at any place of diplomacy.

Department Stores

If you are planning to spend a significant amount of time in Paris, try to find a local department store as soon as possible. Think of how many times, domestically, you run errands during any given week, and consider that once you have established a routine in Paris, these errands will become commonplace. Parisian department stores are no different from American department stores, except seeing the lower lines of high-end designers at the Sears equivalent takes a little getting used to. Hypothetically, if the dry cleaner has not lived up to your lofty expectations, finding an iron in Paris is possible as well. A few recommended department stores to consider are:

BHV
52-64, rue de Rivoli,
Paris, France 75004
Tel: +33.42.74.90.00
Web: www.bhv.fr

C & A
49, Boulevard Haussmann
75009 Paris.
Tel: +33.53.30.89.33
Web: www.c-et-a.fr

Monoprix
(numerous locations
throughout Paris)
Web: www.monoprix.fr

Finding a Safe Place for *Europe Beyond Your Means: Paris Edition*

Remember this sage advice: you can always secure an additional passport, but finding a copy of this invaluable tool in Paris may prove difficult. Paris is famous for pickpockets, so find a safe hiding place for this book—it's one the best decisions you can make.

Truly, no amount of preparation is too much, but because *Beyond Your Means* travelers balk at the idea of preparing, keeping in mind the points mentioned here will be invaluable to your settling in.

5

"One Night in Paris"

When planning nights out, it is important to consider all possibilities and directions the evening could take. First and foremost, Parisian nightlife is legendary. Despite the rampant availability of elitist bars with overpriced drinks, a night out in Paris can be whatever you want it to be. Essentially, any club or bar experience can be had, ranging from an exclusive evening at Hotel Costes to an obnoxious sing-a-long at a dive bar.

Paris has much to offer, so there is no reason to limit your evenings out, especially since *Beyond Your Means* travelers are equally comfortable in all settings. Trust-fund babies are able to drink their nights merrily away with the other pewter-pot pilferers on Rue Oberkampf, while middle-class pseudo-intellectuals are able to appear rich and bored while sipping champagne in the garden at the Ritz. As long as your credit and conscience hold out, the disguise is yours for the duration of your stay. This idea harkens back to choosing your character for the trip, with a *Beyond Your Means* traveler's chameleon-like suavity, switching roles and fitting in anywhere is possible and encouraged.

As *Europe Beyond Your Means* has emphasized, compared to other nations, the French excel at lavishness and luxury like an Orange County girl on her Super Sweet 16. Therefore, Paris can easily provide whatever it is you want to do that requires at least four stars, white tablecloths, and servers in three-piece uniforms. Conversely, Paris is also a city with plenty of seedy options that can nourish the Freudian *ids* in all of us. Overall, there are four types of evenings that you could plan in Paris: an Elite Evening, a Romp through Paris, an Observer's Night, and the Complete Tourist Evening.

No matter the type of evening you plan, the best *Beyond Your Means* approach is to spread all activities out across the city, with absolutely no regard for linear progression. Taking a taxi at every opportunity is essential. As you crisscross the city after dark, zipping down roads like Voie Georges Pompidou on the Right Bank, you and any companions will be more than impressed by the inspiring beauty of the framed and illuminated museums, bridges, churches, and all other random buildings introducing themselves with Ionic or Corinthian columns. What could possibly be more *Beyond Your Means* than recklessly taking a cab back and forth across the same routes, with the fares mounting exclusively for art's sake?

Before jumping into a little car with a green light on top, consider the exact type of evening you are planning so that you can dress appropriately and set the proper wheels in motion.

"Then Let Them Eat Cake ... " a.k.a., an Elite Evening

There are no limits to the assorted "theme evenings" that can be had. Given the prevalence of jet-setters and hipsters who want to "do Paris," a good starting point is to consider a theme evening that would most attract such a crowd.

Mastering the Nightlife Social Hierarchy

Between dinner, drinks, and whatever else may ensue, a high-end evening will certainly provide a great opportunity to observe the lifestyle of the world's rich and famous. Countless revolutions aside, the argument can be made that France, especially Paris, is still very much divided into social classes.

Paris still has somewhat of a "rich/beautiful" versus "poor/student" divide. These are not exact guidelines, though. For instance, you will find plenty of middle-class patrons mixing with the very rich at many of the city's discotheques on any given night. But like most examples of social divide, the separation is more self-imposed than intentionally inflicted. A sense of entitlement and enough cash to last for the evening can take a faker very far. To borrow a concept from *Midnight in the Garden of Good and Evil*, one can be *nouveau riche*, "but then again, it's the *riche* part that counts."

All this being said, unless tourists carry titles from deposed monarchies, they have little importance in the classist chess game that may or may not be going on inside certain bars, nightclubs, bistros, or in *la rue*. To master the caste system that is Parisian nightlife, *Beyond Your Means* travelers should pay even less accord to the ascribed roles of pawn or knight because of their unique abilities regarding social disguise. When temporary acceptance is key, skills like masking your true financial wherewithal by unmitigated overpurchasing prove to be invaluable. After all, *Beyond Your Means* travelers are just as well known for making calls on behalf of suspended credit cards as they are for claiming to be three-quarters through their most recent novel.

How to Begin an Elite Evening

Parisians almost always have a pre-dinner cocktail called an *apéritif*. This does not limit you to having one at the restaurant where you've chosen to dine. Of course, having a cocktail elsewhere in no way limits you from having another at a future destination. We've often had more than just one. Swanky hotel bars, like one you may be staying at (or at least pretending to), or upscale cafés on any of the major boulevards are always a safe bet. While the bus tour patrons are trudging through another sixteenth-century cathedral, good *Beyond Your Means* practitioners spend their days memorizing the names of chic and tantalizing bars to which they can return later during their adventures.

This is the time to conjure up those memories of where you saw that café that looked to be *Beyond Your Means*. Have a *Kir* or *Kir Royal*, and get the grandiloquent evening underway—Parisian style. After this quasi-necessary first step, you can consider heading to your intended *schloss* of sustenance for dinner.

The Importance of Dinner to an Elite Evening

Thoughts on eating have permeated this guide extensively, but it is such a key component to French culture that it must be discussed in different capacities. The finer points of *Beyond Your Means* dining are discussed elsewhere, but there are a few other issues that particularly pertain to high-end dining, which must be emphasized.

- Reservations are always required. In upscale Parisian restaurants, reservations are needed any day of the week. Just to prove a point, *maître d'*s will happily send walk-ins away, even if the restaurant is half-full. This methodology and suspended laws of economics come from the same line of thinking that prevents field horses from being allowed in the stalls at the Kentucky Derby. Of course, if you arrive much earlier than the dinner crowd or after the important clientele have already left, you might be offered a table as a walk-in, but *Beyond Your Means* travelers usually have no interest in eating dinner during "the early bird special" or at nearly midnight. Besides, being seen is part of the reason for going. What's the point in spending money you don't have to see a lesser show at the same price? To ensure you're offered the same experience, one should book a table at least five hours ahead, if not a day or two before.

- Trust in thy chef. All smaller restaurants in Paris, exclusive or otherwise, invariably have a three-course special menu for the evening. This will usually include about three choices for each course. Understand that this is not the equivalent to a seasonal "summer fajitas" menu you might find at home. Whatever the chef is specializing in that evening, which means it changes every day, is well worth consideration. Non-French–speaking *Beyond Your Means* travelers may especially want to heed this advice. While tag-a-long members of your party are attempting to translate the whole menu with French-English dictionaries, you'll be able to salvage those valuable minutes reconciling one or two items from the special menu. You will also obviously appear more local by signaling to others that you have full faith in the ability of a Parisian chef to decide what it is you should eat, rather than going through the tiresome work of choosing yourself.

- Crème Brûlée—No Way!: When ordering dessert, remember that requesting a *crème brûlée* can be considered insulting to the chef. In France, this is like saying, "You're food was horrible. You did nothing right. I can't believe I have to pay to eat here. Maybe if I just ask you to make the easiest dessert in the world, at least you won't screw that up." Therefore, order the "burnt cream" with caution. Usually, it's assumed that foreigners do not know this rule, so when *Bertrand* the chef has a word with the waiter and inquires why someone ordered a *crème brûlée*, the information will probably just be relayed that you're *un étranger*.

The Next Step

After you've settled on having a bourgeois evening, finished your long dinner, and had the obligatory coffee, start looking for another place to wear away a little more of that black strip on your cash card. If you're really in for the long Parisian evening, you'll need to look bored somewhere between the hours of 11:00 p.m. and 1:00 a.m. There is no real magical equation to this step; to be honest, it is really only a repeat of the first cocktail that started the evening. The same general rules apply, but this time, try to seem more sultry. When planning your after dinner events, consider that:

- *Kir* or *Kir Royal* would be sort of silly after dinner.

- Going somewhere that you just heard about through eavesdropping at dinner is completely acceptable.

- The French generally go out rather late, so don't put the pedal down on the alcohol accelerator too early in the night, or you'll miss out on potential adventures. Public drunkenness is also not as appreciated in Paris as it is after a Fiesta Bowl victory, so you might as well just go home if you become legless at any time.

- *Beyond Your Means* is in no position to recommend which clubs are most suitable—this, after all, is just as fickle an industry as fashion. Remember, though, the best policy is to book a table ahead of time. You don't want to be caught outside in the line of people who don't stand a chance of getting in. Tables do present minimums, but with a healthy-sized troupe and a little magic from the folks at Visa, you'll be just fine.

An Attempted Look Back at L'Hôtel Costes.

As we entered the Hotel Costes, I found myself wondering if a truck outside had struck my entourage. It seemed, by the lack of attention we were given, that maybe only our spirits had somehow wandered into the foyer of this venerable establishment. The abrupt change when entering this amphitheater of artistic luxury, with its soft red light on black marble, compared to the dirty street outside, made it no easier to feign belonging at this royal court of decadence. Attempting to cover a sudden onset of meekness with papier-mâché masks of confidence, we approached the hostess podium and stood directly in front of it. For some reason, we couldn't seem to make eye contact with any of the working femme fatales standing less than a foot away. Other patrons walked right through us as if our bodies were merely hinged to doorframes. They received pleasant receptions and the attention of multiple hostesses on the way to their tables, leaving me to wonder if my original premonition had indeed been correct. As I was soon to find out, we were present but just didn't exist at that moment, as far as the hostesses were concerned. Being turned away at a velvet rope would have been much less insulting, but like a lot of things in Paris, giving up out of pride is what they expect. We needed to endure.

The Hotel Costes was selected that evening at the urging of a member of the group who wanted a "classier" night out on la ville. Admittedly, the only thing I'd known about it beforehand was that, along with Buddha Bar, it produced its own lounge CDs every year that became the "vogue" music of choice for female Ivy League medical-school grads trying to diversify and smarten up their music collection. I came to learn later that it was also a "den of opulence" that stood up to its "everything in excess" reputation.

Still suffering the indignity that my personal decoration of designer jeans, a white button-down oxford, and a linen sports coat didn't make a passing grade, I moved ever closer to the hostess, who had no choice but to acknowledge our party. After all, we were now blocking the entrance to the bar and restaurant. Sighing dismissively while rolling her eyes, she asked how many we'd be. Thinking that we'd succeeded, a chase followed suit behind her toward a new location. She tried to lose us by capitalizing on our ignorance of the route and her above-average foot speed, but we kept our pace brisk and the gap close.

She hurried us past the candlelit tables and chic diners in the hotel's famous courtyard café to a smaller section reserved for those just having drinks. We entered a room with high ceilings, a multitude of cocktail tables, and posh leather chairs, where French rap moguls sat with thin white models, and wealthy French businessmen entertained their mistresses over champagne-based cocktails. Finally, we thought we'd be given our just deserts in the form of an actual seat at the party, but the hostess had no such intention. She merely dumped us near the entrance of the bar. This is where our real trial began, making our first test seem like a paltry arraignment.

We stood in the main foot-traffic lines, where we were told to wait and were forced to utter the phrase "pardonnez moi" every six seconds to the bar's other customers. All the while, scantily clad waitresses perpetually shuffled by us, retrieving drinks for their customers, annoyed at our impediment to their work and our general existence.

Seemingly, the point here is to see how much you deserve a seat in their cocktail lounge—to see how imperturbable or nonchalant you can be. A trial meant to judge your worth and discover if you and your cohorts should be allowed to stay before finally gaining their approval. Certainly not a trial that our American sensibilities were accustomed to, as there was no jury of our peers but a jury of those who viewed themselves as our superiors.

After what seemed like an eternity, we were eventually acquitted of our social misfortune and offered seats in the far back corner, which we were only too glad to receive, as it allowed us to finally get out from under the stares of the other patrons. We'd endured, but what had we really won?

The answer to that question came slowly but without warning. After the near-eternity that passed between our seating and a drinks menu being offered, our winnings became obvious. The prizes that evening were to be €30 martinis and dismissive table service.

Costes flaunts attitude and affluence like Versailles flaunts gold decorative leaves, but after around €60 worth of the clear panoply from the Nordic states, none of that mattered anymore. All the social judgment seemed to fade comfortably to the rear, the way it often does after a few heart-starters. We paid our bill and strode proudly out past the overweight rap moguls and the middle-aged businessmen. It seemed to me, but most probably only in my mind's eye, that as we left, a few of the cocktail waitresses nodded toward us in approval for our accomplishment of social endurance. A random hostess in the marble hallway might have even smiled to me on the way out.

Then again, this must have been imaginary; such acknowledgment would be mal à propos at the Hotel Costes.

Getting into the Club

Capitalizing on a *Beyond Your Means* traveler's ability to mingle with just about anyone is important, but you may also want to try using the following techniques to assist:

- Call Ahead: While this is a rule for anywhere for anything, this isn't the type of calling ahead required to get one of the priority tables at Outback Steakhouse. While it is a difficult task, it's always worth a shot to call ahead and pretend to be the personal representative for a United States senator or a member of the British Parliament, whose family would like a table in the corner for the evening. Do this with the caveat that the actual family of that individual may also be requesting the same table. Also, be prepared to explain that the senator or MP himself had an urgent meeting at the embassy and therefore will not be dining with the rest of his party.

- Dress the Part: As a *Beyond Your Means* traveler, you don't own Pumas or anything else that is humiliating, but doing your research beforehand and ensuring that you look the part will help your cause. Remember that "celebutantes" and rock stars can get away with certain looks that the average poser cannot. After all, this isn't San Francisco; conformity will help you gain credibility.

- Cool Assertiveness: Even if you feel a bit out of place, it is important to never look so. Remember that lions always trounce on the weak. Don't expect the same approach and greeting from the staff at a chic Paris bar as you would at Cracker Barrel, thus making a beeline for the hostess to request a seat will aid your cause. Provided you are cool and collected while maintaining an air of entitlement, the gatekeepers may see you as one of their own and deserving acknowledgment.

- Avoid Sneaking In: There are countless pointers (and even TV specials) dedicated to teaching people how to crash a party or how to slip in the private celebrity entrance of exclusive gatherings by pretending to be with the guest of honor. Don't try. Laymen's success rate of these techniques is very low. Consider that someone in Madonna's entourage will realize you aren't part of it, and the embarrassment could be enough to ruin your time—and getting physically thrown out could scuff the Bruno Maglis you purchased for the evening.

Eventually, success will be had by gaining access to some of Paris' exclusive social clubs and capping off your elite Parisian evening. But despite Paris' reputation as a very expensive city, there is no need to limit your evenings to only those experiences that max out credit cards.

Romping through Paris

Paris shouldn't only be associated with white tablecloths, pretentious waiters, aloof hostesses, and a "no room at the inn" mentality. Paris is also a place where your class can be checked at the door. To illustrate this point, take a *Beyond Your Means* favorite as an example: *Au Refuge des Fondus*. This Montmartre legend is not a favorite for its glitz and glamour but rather for the inexpensive indulgence it offers.

A place like *Au Refuge des Fondus* can be found tucked into one of many long, winding streets still prevalent in Montmartre. Such neighborhoods still exist in Montmartre because Haussmann's reforms never reached what was then outside of Paris. The façade of *Au Refuge des Fondus* looks jolly enough, if not a little beaten. There is often a shock when first entering the establishment, followed by an urge for immediate retreat, as the incredibly close quarters are no more than the size of a truck trailer backed into a building, with picnic tables set up, one after another, on each wall.

It seems, at first glance, that the room is too small; there aren't places available; the food probably isn't that good; or it's not your type of crowd. None of above, however, is true (well, the food isn't exactly the best in Paris, but that's not their shtick anyway). The wood-paneled walls tell a story of the type of people who have come through the small threshold on *rue des Trois Frères* and made themselves patrons. They are literally covered with carvings that read "Dartmouth," "McGill," "Mike—'99," "101st," or whatever else you can possibly imagine. There is basically a 100 percent chance that you'll find the name of your university or even someone you know carved into the wall.

The seating, as stated before, is super-tight—you will be sitting as close to strangers as you will to members of your own party, but after a few gulps from the baby bottles filled with wine, which are served nonstop during dinner, the proximity to strangers will no longer matter. Nursing from the teat of Bacchus always does wonders to reduce the need for personal space.

Despite knowing the address, you may still get lost trying to find the restaurant because of the obscurity of so many establishments in Montmartre; thus, you ostensibly will be hungry by the time you arrive. Fear not, though;

the food arrives quite quickly after you are seated. The *apéritif* and *entrée* come almost immediately, giving your table the time to decide which type of fondue (cheese or meat or both) you might fancy.

Drunken revelers fondue for hours, drink heavily from their baby bottles, and have been known to sing songs to each other or to other tables. Many parties play the restaurant's standard game that if someone drops bread or meat in the fondue pot, that person will be forced to entertain the table— and the restaurant, for that matter—with a song of his or her choice. The debauchery can be followed up in typical French style, with dessert, coffee, and a cognac, running about €35 to €45 a person.

Au Refuge des Fondus is never short on characters. Real artists still living, working, and hocking in the Montmartre area sit next to the same pedigrees present in any of the most white-shoe New York law firms. *Beyond Your Means* practitioners should take advantage of the situation and try to show their true breadth for internationalism in Paris. Lines like "I know this little fondue restaurant up in the 11th—kind of dodgy, but it's really fun" will easily score you points with any self-proclaimed "up for anything" group. Some travelers may use their time at *Au Refuge des Fondus* as an opportunity to show that they too can loosen up and have fun, while others might be trying to show their cohorts that it is possible to have an outrageous, big boozy meal in Paris for not a lot of money.

A word of caution: always be prepared to sing a few lines *a capella*, as even the most experienced fondue-dipper will drop a tasty morsel at least once and be required to entertain. As a result, you will notice the true international flair that is Paris, while being entertained with everything from Irish drinking songs to French rock to the latest that Nashville has to offer. If you are interested:

Au Refuge des Fondus
17 rue des Trois Frères
Tel. +33.42.55.22.65
Contrary to popular belief, it does take reservations. Going with a group is suggested.

Continuing to Romp

If looking to continue your evening with good ol' inebriation, there are various paths to take. There is always *Les Halles* as an option. Here, there are a string of bars anchored by *Café Rue Doite*, just off Place Joachim du Bellay on the extra-seedy and extra-dirty Rue Saint Denis. But bear in mind that you'll be sipping your Stellas while toothless prostitutes proposition you from the sidewalk. Nothing in this area, including the prostitutes, can be classified as *Beyond Your Means*.

Therefore, if you're in Paris, and your main goal for the evening is to get over-served, then you basically have two viable options: 1) visit a famous string of hard-drinking bars on Rue Oberkampf with a distinctly French flavor; or 2) go with what you already know, understand, and love by visiting the various cafés and bars in the 6th with more Anglophone leanings.

Oberkampf: French for "Booze Alley"

There are plenty of classic Anglo-Irish pubs all throughout Paris, but you won't find these ale embassies with any concentrated presence on Rue Oberkampf. What separates this potential bar crawl from many of the other routes around town is that it is decidedly French in nature. One can venture from *belle-époque* at *Café Charbon* to DJ bars touting Latin-influenced salsa music, like *La Maizon*. Because Oberkampf is so diverse, so boho-French, and so non-American, it is *Beyond Your Means* gold. While other tourists are plotting their next souvenir shot-glass purchase at the Hard Rock Café, *Beyond Your Means* practitioners will be enveloped in "intoxicating" conversation with French socialists.

The main scene takes place on the long, narrow part of the street west of the *Parmentier Métro* and Avenue de la République on the aforementioned street itself. Notably, not quite as close to the *Oberkampf Métro* as one might think. There is plenty of variety to keep even the biggest scene queens occupied the whole evening. No matter where you start or what you favor, those still standing after 2:00 a.m. usually end up leaning into a beer at *Quartier General*. Other than on the weekends, *Quartier General* is the only bar open after this ill-fated hour, making it a magnet for those far too serious to go to work or school the next day. It basically serves as the Parisian version of a hole-in-the-wall drinker's bar, with the committed proprietors serving the 2:00 a.m. to 4:00 a.m. crowd, regardless of what day it is.

Though this is not a hard-and-fast itinerary, here are four *Beyond Your Means* favorites in Oberkampf—but bear in mind there are many more bars on *la rue*.

- Chez Justine: 96 Rue Oberkampf, +33.43.57.44.03

- Charbon: 109 Rue Oberkampf, +33.43.57.55.13. The original and probably the best bar on the street.

- La Maizon: 123 Rue Oberkampf, +33.58.30.61.12. Saturday and Sunday open until 6:00 a.m.

- Quartier General: 101-103 Rue Oberkampf, +33.43.14.65.78. French version of a hole-in-the-wall bar. Open until 4:00 a.m. every night of the week and therefore will get crowded when the other bars on *la rue* shut earlier on weekdays.

Although Rue Oberkampf is the main artery of the bar scene, there are equally deserving establishments on any of the roads, both perpendicular and parallel, to the main drag. While discussing adventures in Oberkampf, *Beyond Your Means* travelers might want to keep lines like "I really liked Oberkampf before, but it's just gotten too popular and run-out these days" in their verbal arsenals. Consider also using "I prefer the bars on Rue Saint Maur and Rue Jean Pierre Timbaud to start the evening," and the ever-popular "Of course, I like to hang out on Oberkampf, too, but usually only after most of the 'Tanqueray Tourists' have gone home."

The Channel-Crossing Pub Crawl

Despite being historical rivals in everything from economics to world domination, there is a large British presence in France; thus, bars that cater to the Limey set are plentiful. Such establishments make up the nucleus of Anglophone ex-pat life in Paris, where you will find plenty of Irish and British youth working on their gap years before university. As part of any romp through Paris, preparation for an evening pub crawl should include ample sleep, until about noon or preferably after. You should then assemble your squad some time in the late afternoon and start crafting your evening.

One option is to start out near Saint-Michel on the Rue Saint-André des Arts. You'll be able to find plenty of local establishments that might seem more at home in Europe's northwest isles as the street progresses toward the intersection of Rue Mazarine and Rue de Buci. Stop in for a less-than-icy-cold Strongbow or Guinness, and even try the shepherd's pie, if you're feeling a little famished. From there, you should consider following Rue de Buci until the intersection with Boulevard Saint-Germain. This section of the tour is slightly different than the previous street; meaning you shouldn't have any trouble finding establishments specializing in Catholic communions. This is where one changes bottles and "crosses the channel."

At the end of the road you'll find the famous *Café Mabillon*, and since you'll probably already be feeling a little more than generous and your pallet totally numbed, you should feel free to splurge on a bottle of the bubbly.

After all, you deserve it. The waiters at *Mabillon* are smartly dressed, and the clientele will be more than a minor elevation from where you started. Just don't expect fast service from the "seen your kind before" wait staff.

After settling up with your waiter, you could hang a right at Boulevard Saint-Germain. After about one real block, you will pass all the oh-so-popular places—*Café de Flore* and *Les Deux Magots*, which aren't really worth the stop. They're also filled with American sightseers who once read Hemmingway in high school and heard that he used to frequent the joint. Needless to say, the quarter and the cafés aren't quite like they were in 1930. They have now become the kind of places you wouldn't want to patronize during a bar crawl.

Since it will be getting late by this point, and certain members of your group may have already wandered off, you should head to any of the large and infamous Australian-American-Irish-English-Scottish-Canadian bars that are right in that area already. In fact, if you are incredibly devilish you just might want to do a complete tour of only these bars in a single evening. Depending on the list, this could easily be a ten-bar destination in and of itself, all within one square mile.

If you are having trouble planning your exact route, or you just want a few suggestions along the way, below is a pre-planned Anglo bar crawl that won't disappoint:

Anglophone Bar Crawl

The Outback 42 rue du Cardinal Lemoine 75005 Paris Tel: +33.43.54. 30.48	→	Bombardier Pub 2 Place De Pantheon 75005 Tel: +33.43.54 .79.22	→	Le Violon Dingue 46 Rue Montagne Sainte Geneviève 75005 Tel : +33.43.25.79. 93
← ↓	Pub St. Michel 19 Quai St. Michel 75005 Tel: +33.46.33.30.41	←	The Long Hop 27 Rue Frédéric Sauton 75005 Tel: +33.43.29 .40.54	↓ ←
Corcoran's Irish Pub 28 rue St. Andre des Arts 75006 Tel: +33.40.46. 97.46	→	The Mazet 61 rue St. Andre Des Arts 75006 Tel: +33.43.25 .57.50	→	The Highlander 8 rue de Nevers 75006 Tel: +33.43.26. 54.20

END	The Frog & Princess 9 rue Princesse, 75006 Tel : +33.40.51.77.38	←	The Moosehead 16 rue des Quatres Vents 75006 Tel: +33.46.33 77.00	↓ ←

No matter what your own personal bar-crawl itinerary says, *Beyond Your Means* travelers are warned to stay away from what foreigners always think is the "Latin Quarter." These are the small, windy streets near the river and west of *Métro St. Michel*. Yes, you will be able to find plenty of Anglo places to drink, but this spot competes for "top tourist trap in the city," year after year. Many tourists think it's the *actual* Latin Quarter because the streets are pedestrian-traffic only, very old, and cobblestoned. The reality is that the Latin Quarter is only named such because of the students at the nearby *La Sorbonne*, who spoke Latin in their courses. This section is no more "Latin," with its T-shirt shops and lifeless drinking establishments, than any other section of the 5th arrondissement and has more of a "Disney Presents Main Street USA" feel than any type of authentic experience.

An Observer's Night

If your goal for the post-dinner evening isn't necessarily to forget what you did but instead to do some people-watching, a good place to consider might be somewhere like *Le Fumoir*. It is and has historically been, as the name suggests, a temple to the black arts: smoking. It's on the south side of the Louvre, which serves as the perfect backdrop for you to consider which Sartre novel you're going to purchase and pretend to read. That is, of course, if you're able to keep your eyes and intellect focused on literary works with the preponderance of European models, both men and women, sauntering across the floor, dragging on their Yves Saint-Laurent cigarettes. *Le Fumoir*, however, should be kept separate from your romp through Paris, as it isn't an Irish bar, and it's just not the kind of place to let your frat flag fly. Besides, no one ever heard of the Psi Kappa chapter at *La Sorbonne*.

To see it for yourself:

Le Fumior
6 Rue de l'amiral Coligny
75001 (behind *Le Louvre*)
Tel. +33.42.92.00.24
Web: www.lefumoir.com

After a couple of cocktails and your muse now in full gear, you'll be ready to stroll down the boulevards or bridges that frame Paris' architectural wonders. Parisians love to walk after dinner and drinks. Doing so not only allows them to work off a few of the extra calories while enjoying the abject beauty of their city, but it also provides them the opportunity to ponder their own superiority to the rest of the world.

The Complete Tourist Evening

We have provided suggestions for different types of evenings and ways to observe the culture, but the most highly recommended option is to discover Paris for yourself. Not only will this help you to become an independent expert on Paris and the French, but excess aside, *Beyond Your Means* travelers seek to appear more locally educated in their evenings out than anything else. Anyone can go to the Ritz or any of the other expensive and famous places and spend a diamond mine's worth of euros. But savvy *Beyond Your Means* travelers are more interested in actually fooling others into thinking they know the hidden gems not quite on the radar of the Michelin Guide.

This being the case, Paris couldn't be more perfect. It is quite possibly one of the easiest cities in the world in which to just walk around and do nothing but sip espresso and stumble on some place to *mange*. Whether it's wandering the side streets behind the *Palace des Vosges* in the 4th or walking around the 8th, 16th, or 17th, Paris has no shortage of cafés, bistros, or brasseries that eclipse the quality of food you'll find back home at culinary epicenters like The Cheesecake Factory.

Paris can be the most exciting city in the world, but it is up to travelers to experience the city for themselves with a variety of individual experiences. The only balancing test is whether to have the elite evenings early or late in your trip. There is thought that supports waiting to the end so that you don't run out of money early, but *Beyond Your Means* travelers should be self-actualized enough to know that they can't wait that long.

6

When in Rome ... or Paris, That Is

...

The "Teen Tour"

The final leg of a two-week venture to Europe was just beginning. After twelve straight days of touring Houses of Parliament, Westminster Abbey, the Hofbrauhaus, a Venetian glass factory, the Palace of Schonbrunn, unnoticed continental capitals, and everywhere else mentioned in National Lampoon's European Vacation, we entered the city of Paris. The trip up to this point had been too jam-packed with sights to be culturally rewarding. On a tour bus full of giddy fifteen-year-olds, my fellow adolescents were armed with video games and had playing cards firmly in hand. "Europe" had become merely a different backdrop to our regular lives. The countless games of "I Spy" had no doubt annoyed the French tour guide, but he appeared unfazed, as he likely developed a high tolerance for the amusements of American fifteen-year-olds after guiding a new batch of anxious teens through a Cliffs Notes version of Europe every few weeks.

There were not enough teens to legitimize our own exclusive bus, so the tour company had "logically" decided it should rent out space on the bus to cover costs. The bus was fully occupied by thirty teens, their chaperones, guides, two large families, three Mormon missionaries, and a few retirees anxious to visit rather fabled places that the pubertal crowd in the back of the imposing vehicle couldn't yet appreciate. Our fellow bus-riding comrades were less than amused by our high-school banter; but by around day eleven, they too acquiesced to the addictive temptation of annoying the leaders of the tour with excessive and repetitive questions.

The bus barreled through the crowded city streets of Paris en route to yet another hotel for a two-day stint. Even the exclusively French speaking bus driver seemed to grow a bit weary at the countless comments of "look how small their cars are." However, the monotony of the situation was soon broken by the sudden shriek from a girl wearing a sweatshirt emblazoned with "#54's girlfriend." Her startled exclamation led the entire bus to look in her direction as she pointed to the right side of our sixty-seated chariot. Suddenly, sounds of "Oh, my God" and "Ew-w" turned to laughter, once all riders saw that she was pointing at a twenty-something man who had chosen to relieve himself by a tree on a side street. The man, who was careful to conceal his delivery mechanism, noticed the commotion and gave the bus a head-nod, slight wave, and a bashful smile. As the crowd stared in awe, an older gentleman on the bus from North Carolina, sporting a cap adorned with WWII buttons, stated with authority, "That is not uncommon! That is not uncommon in Europe!" However, the attempted lesson on cultural acceptance was lost on "#54's girlfriend" and the rest of the teen-tour audience. This being the first time such a sight had been witnessed by the collective group, the school-required travel journals were feverishly retrieved and pens went flying in order to record this "special" memory.

Despite all the wonderful sites seen in this whirlwind adventure, upon returning to school, this story was perhaps the most shared. Others admired with awe at the newly cultured world travelers, once we returned to homeroom with our photos of Europe's highlights, including the man engaged in a common, necessary bodily function. Since that time, some members of the class have become veterans of Mardi Gras celebrations or made frequent trips through the subway systems of major cities and may now view public urination as no longer warranting notice. However, for that brief moment in time, this isolated Parisian spectacle entered into the shared memories of an entire sophomore class, especially #54's girlfriend.

After figuring out where everything is in your neighborhood and running to the local BHV to pick up the items you inevitably forgot to pack or that weren't high enough on the priority list to include in your luggage, the time comes to figure out exactly what to do in Paris.

When traveling to Paris in the *Beyond Your Means* style, it shouldn't necessarily be assumed that every tourist landmark has already been visited. Many travelers may have visited a few token destinations at some point during a quick ten-day teen tour of Europe, but all have not. You'll remember these rapid tours of the old country as the ones where your mom made sure to review the itinerary beforehand, the French club advisor had to get special approval from the Board of Education, and everyone on the trip was fascinated by the soft-core porn (meaning *sans* "money shot") on local European television. However, if somehow you missed this trip during high school or college, make sure to visit these places, because there are reasons why they are included on every stock tour of the French capital.

Predictably, *Beyond Your Means* travelers may turn up their noses at the idea of being seen in places where American-style English is the dominant language, but the jewels of Paris are probably worthy of your consideration. This will provide the perfect medium to experiment with canned statements like "the view from the Eiffel Tower is breathtaking," while actually being able to speak from experience. Besides, if you have yet to choose which persona to embrace when in Paris, this will provide an unprecedented opportunity to further ponder your options and practice a heavy European accent and aloof attitude, while giving poor directions to others.

At this point in your scholarship, certain reminders may not be necessary, but it is imperative to remember that no matter the location, a traveler must at least look the part of a *Beyond Your Means* practitioner. As discussed previously, flip-flops or T-shirts with pictures of French landmarks are the equivalent of wearing an "I Love New York" T-shirt in the Big Apple or posing for a picture with your hands on the cement where your favorite star once stood in Hollywood.

The "Check-Offs"

Places like the Eiffel Tower, *Arc de Triomphe*, and Notre Dame Cathedral are all examples of sites that can easily be referred to as "check-offs." Visit them to check them off a list, and don't go back unless there is a compelling reason to do so, like the ice cream near Notre Dame. Of course, anything of personal interest is a high priority, but equally important is the ability to speak with authority about a popular destination when back home. There is inherent value for a *Beyond Your Means* traveler in being able to offer authoritative suggestions like "I was out of breath when walking up the steps to the *Sacré-Cœur*, so I highly recommend taking the tram." Thus, making an allowance for places that are important to others should be a consideration as well. When planning a time to visit the "check-offs," the best bet is to use one of two approaches, depending on your interest level: the "quick-and-easy" approach or the "thorough" approach.

The "Quick-and-Easy" Approach

This particular approach generally condenses the "check-offs" into about one day. The most highly recommended quick-and-easy method is to crawl out of bed as early as possible—at least before noon—and start on a personal mission. This tactic provides the most flexibility and can be the least expensive, thus preserving cash flow for the more important indulgences, like eating and drinking. Granted, as every *Beyond Your Means* traveler is different, this could also be an endeavor where you choose to make a major investment.

There are numerous travel companies in Paris that specialize in organizing day trips for just such adventures, so many options exist to lose a lot of euros on a "check-off" day. These companies vary in their services, with some providing relatively inexpensive walking tours and others providing a car service or a combination of walking and riding. If considering a quick-and-easy approach where you are willing to invest some capital, consult any of these services, depending on your needs and preferences. Note that many charge different prices for different vehicles, and it goes without saying that riding in a Mercedes is a more expensive tour than hopping on a bus. For further information, check out the following:

www.travelswithfriends.com/Private_Driver-Guides_in_Paris.htm
www.frenchadventures.com
www.parisluxurytours.com
www.frenchlinks.com
www.pariswalkabout.com
www.yachtsdeparis.fr

But the tried-and-true method of "quick and easy" is to limit the number of times you hit the snooze button, buy a *carte orange* for the day, and handle everything on your own. Be sure to pick up a brochure at each spot to learn the interesting factoids that will make you the centerpiece of many cocktail parties. The following examples are classic "check-off" activities worthy of your consideration:

- **The Eiffel Tower**. You just have to. This international symbol of Paris is easily described without visiting, but no travel guide, not even a *tra-vella*, can encourage skipping it. The Eiffel Tower opens in the morning at 9:00, but bear in mind that all visitors to Paris will try to make it there eventually and likely will want to start their days at this location. Consider saving this to the end of your "check-off" period, as it is open until 11:00 p.m. or midnight, depending on the time of year, and the lines diminish as evening sets in. If you choose to make this a destination where your get in touch with your tourist-self, don't worry; this is certainly one place in Paris where no one will judge you for ordering a funnel cake. *Closest métro stop:* Bir-Hakeim or Champ de Mars-Tour Eiffel

- **Notre Dame Cathedral**. This is the one Notre Dame where there will be no mention of football, the four horsemen, or the glory days. Instead of praying to a pigskin, this has been a site of Catholic worship for approximately one thousand years. This may be a good place to begin the day, as everyone else will be at the Eiffel Tower. The climb up the 387 stairs to the top of the towers is worth it, but try to resist the standard quips of the less creative: "Has anyone seen the hunchback?" *Closest métro stop:* Cité

- **Arc de Triomphe**. This example of Napoleonic power is quite a sight, if you can avoid being struck by a car while trying to access it. France's unknown soldier is buried here, where an eternal flame has burned continuously under the archway since 1921 in memory of all who died in World War I. On July 2, 1998, however, the flame was momentarily extinguished when a drunken Mexican soccer fan urinated on it—not kidding (look it up). It is also worth a stop because it is right at the end of another "check-off," the Champs-Élysées. *Closest métro stop:* George V

- **Champs-Élysées**. As one of the most famous streets in the world, "Elysian Fields," as it translates, deserves a walk. Plan to combine this with your visit to the *Arc de Triomphe*. Unfortunately, this storied location is now the site of such exotic locations as Planet Hollywood, but it is still worth a stroll.

- **Sacré-Cœur**. Most pre-packaged tours of Europe will include too many churches and cathedrals, but this is one that is worth a visit, if for no other reason than to have a connection with the girls back home who went to the local "Sacred Heart" Academy. It is a hefty hike up too many stairs to count, so consider the tram alternative. *Closest métro stop:* Anvers

- **La Bastille**. Make your old Western Civ teacher proud by heading over to *La Bastille*. The French love to riot and protest, and the events here started it all. This is also in an area known for its nightlife, so a quick visit can dovetail into other more important activities. *Closest métro stop:* Bastille

- **Pantheon**. A lot of really neat dead people are buried here. From Voltaire to Marie Curie, this is a crypt where many people important to France and the world are entombed. Often referred to as the "Critics Crypt" by those less fond of French intellectuals, it is still an impressive structure and worth the price of admission, even if you don't care for the intellectual ramblings of its permanent residents. The Pantheon is located in the Latin Quarter near many other locations that you might want to consider visiting, such as the University of Paris (Sorbonne). *Closest métro stop:* Cardinal-Lemoine

At least a few of these sites should be visited for a good quick-and-easy tour. However, if you have already visited the above locations, use this time for important activities, like locating a neighborhood bar or café that will be the location where everyone will know your name by the end of your stay.

If you're willing to extend the quick-and-easy tour to a day and a half, then venture a few miles outside the city to pay homage to the best example of living beyond your means ever erected: Versailles. With every room at Versailles, you will feel humbled by the work of the quintessential *Beyond Your Means* rulers. Versailles was constructed to house 20,000 individuals, including nobleman, servants, and kings. The rulers who lived there used any and all of the resources in the French empire to take care of each detail. Even after the fall of the Bourbon dynasty, Versailles has remained an important symbol of decadence. To this day, this most impressive structure is occasionally the site of high-level diplomatic functions, the occasional treaty, and really kickin' parties. Visiting Versailles can be an important highlight for a *Beyond Your Means* traveler, as it stands as a perpetual reminder of how remaining slightly within your means is not necessarily a bad thing, if you value your head.

Other Options (a.k.a., the "Thorough Approach")

If following the advice of this guide, you will be spending a large amount of time in Paris; thus, your entire experience should be rather complete. However, the "thorough approach" to hitting the highlights does not necessarily refer to the total trip but could simply be the means used to visit popular locations. As part of this in-depth approach, you may want to pay the few extra euros to hear a guide speak to you about the historical location you are visiting on the quick-and-easy tour. Additionally, the thorough approach can include other important destinations, such as museums and other points of interest.

If spending a great deal of time in Paris then the thorough approach can easily be stretched out for the entire visit, since it isn't possible to do each of these activities in only a day. Ultimately, the best advice for a *Beyond Your Means* traveler is to check-off the necessary activities as soon as possible, whether through the quick-and-easy or thorough approach, so that you can then jump into your chosen persona for the trip and begin making the kind of memories that you will be paying off for the rest of the foreseeable future.

Museums

- **Le Louvre**. While it may seem obvious, a thorough *Beyond Your Means* traveler will visit the Louvre. Of course, it is easy to add the Louvre to the list of "check-offs" by only visiting a few exhibits, including that controversial lady with the puzzling smile. The Louvre was originally the residence of the French monarchy, but the building's boring architecture and cramped space became too *passé* after a number of years, and the Louvre became a lowly museum when the royals moved on to Versailles. Spending significant time at this infamous location will allow a traveler to drop references in conversation to points that only a visitor to the Louvre would know. In keeping with the theme that anything exploited by a movie should be avoided, it is important to be ever watchful of the "Da Vinci Trap." Currently, and potentially until the Rapture, the Louvre—and Paris, in general—are full of *Da Vinci Code* seekers. The book (and now the movie) has stirred up a new interest in French tourism; a *Beyond Your Means* traveler would avoid this level of *fromage* at all costs. Take note that at the Louvre, most every sign is written in basically every language in the Western canon *except* the *Da Vinci Code* tour sign.

These signs are written exclusively in English. A thorough visitor will spend a good bit of time at the Louvre and invest in a guided tour around the museum. *Closest metro stop:* Palais-Royal

- **Musée d'Orsay**. A lot of travel guides will mention this museum as an "off the beaten path" destination, but so many people have found this path that it now has become a "check-off" activity. Thus, a thorough visitor will allow enough time for a visit. While the Louvre is an art lover's Mecca, visiting the *Musée d'Orsay* is a quick way to fill in any gaps. Paris was the birthplace of Impressionism, and the *Musée d'Orsay* is home to many of these great works. Despite their actual opinion, *Beyond Your Means* travelers are always sure to say they prefer the *Musée d'Orsay* because it is "less touristy." Note that when discussing this museum in particular, it is important to remember that it must be called either "*Musée d'Orsay*" or "the Orsay." Saying "*d'Orsay*" by itself translates to "of Orsay," which doesn't sound like someone who knows Paris well. *Closest métro stop:* Solferino.

- **Museum of Your Choice**: In hitting the highlights, a thorough traveler will choose to visit at least one other museum in order to be set apart from the rest of the crowd. Depending on your preference, check out any of the museums dedicated to the works of Picasso, Rodin, other modern art, or just about anything else. Finding an interesting museum in Paris is about as difficult as finding sand in the desert.

An "Authentic Location"

There are so many "must see's" and "must do's" in Paris that tourist traps exist at every juncture. When taking the thorough approach to visiting highlights, *Beyond Your Means* travelers should avoid places that are part of every single stock tour and, instead, find their own location within the same category. Therefore, when asked by friends and relatives if you have visited a certain famous location, your prepared response can be "No, that has gotten so touristy that I had to avoid it. I preferred [insert authentic location here] instead." A couple examples of such activities for the thorough traveler are listed below.

- **Cabarets**. Paris has been famous for cabarets since the days of the original *Chat Noir*. However, thanks to the pioneering efforts of Hollywood, everyone in the world now feels compelled to visit the Moulin Rouge. Yes, the Moulin Rouge may be worth a visit, but when trying to come up with an authentic location, try searching a little bit harder. Paris cabarets are famous, but as a general rule, if there has been a movie made or book dedicated to something, then it has lost a bit of its edge (just ask the regulars at the original Coyote Ugly). Among the best cabarets is *Le Crazy Horse de Paris*, a family-owned cabaret, which is located just off the Champs-Élysées. *Crazy Horse* still maintains a dress code and isn't the type of place to relax standards for those with excuses like "Our bus was late, so we didn't have time to change clothes." The ticket prices range from the approximately €29 for a student-discounted ticket, which restricts a patron to standing by the bar, to the "prestige" dinner-show package, offered with Le Fouquet's restaurant, running approximately €170. The dinner package is truly an exceptional deal, because the food is excellent and comes complete with the dessert of satisfaction in seeing fiscally responsible folks standing at the bar because they were willing to pay only one-fifth of what you did for the exact same entertainment. The show at Crazy Horse has the ability to inspire because it is a genuine celebration of the beautiful female form, making the pole show back home seem lacking. In Crazy Horse's current show, a rather scintillating performance of Eartha Kitt's "Champagne Taste" will encourage any red-blooded man to instantly order an overpriced bottle of Moët & Chandon. As an aside, if inspired to order this famous French beverage at Crazy Horse, keep in mind that the pronunciation is "Mo-et," not "Mo-ay." A sign of a real *Beyond Your Means* traveler is knowing French pronunciations, whether or not one can afford the actual product.

- **Other Notable Cathedrals.** Quite the opposite of the cabaret experience, most stock tours of the city and surrounding region include countless mind-numbing visits to medieval cathedrals. A rule of thumb: once you've seen a couple cathedrals, you've seen them all. Unless gothic architecture or the history of Catholicism is a particular quirky interest, there is no need to visit every possible church. However, since everyone will use basically all cathedral-visiting time at *Notre Dame*, the *Sacré-Cœur*, and *Saint-Chapelle*, fitting in one more notable cathedral will be a great way to have the authentic experience during your thorough approach. The best bet is to find a cathedral that offers some type of musical production or anything other than just the standard brochure and offering plate. For example, a few offer classical music concerts in the evening that are worth checking out. Try visiting *La Abbatiale Saint-Germain-des-Prés* for just such an evening.

- **Napoleon's Tomb** (at Hôtel des Invalides). Originally inspired by St. Peter's Basilica in Rome, this complex actually consists of a number of buildings containing museums and monuments, all relating to the military history of France, as well as a hospital and a retirement home for war veterans, which was the building's original purpose. The French, still disgruntled by the catastrophe at Waterloo, left the little giant buried in remote St. Helena, but after about twenty years they decided that the man who won more military battles than Alexander the Great deserved a proper burial in Paris. In 1861 his body was finally laid to rest in the most prominent location under the dome at Les Invalides.

A Noted "Off-the-Beaten-Path" Location

When visiting highlights, it is important to remember that those who visit Paris and only see a few landmarks often miss the opportunity to tour places that are well known but not as well visited. A way to impress people is by visiting at least one of these locations, even if your itinerary seems constrained. Consider these options:

- **The Catacombs**. Under the city, there are miles and miles of skeletons, placed there at a time when Paris was running out of space for cemeteries and various epidemics were killing people faster than urban planning could handle. However, in the spirit of all things French, there was an attempt to arrange the bones in an artistic manner. Try to avoid the catacombs on the weekend, as only a few people are allowed in at a time and the line can be rather long. Also, take note that backpackers are well aware of this destination; thus, overhearing conversations about how "bitchin' Prague is" or the efficiency of the Eurail youth pass is all but unavoidable. Don't worry, though; backpackers generally fear polo shirts and khakis as a sign of "the Establishment," so they won't approach you.

- **Mosquée de Paris**. Founded after World War I as a sign of France's gratitude to the Muslim *tirailleurs* from the North African colonies who fought against Germany, today it is recognized as a symbol of France's now well-established minority and a center of Muslim worship and culture. The architecture of the building and the open spaces are unique enough to warrant a visit, but be advised that the totality of the structure is not open to inquisitive tourists. Perhaps the most popular thing to do here is enjoy one of the various types of tea offered in the Moorish courtyard.

- **Place to Relax**. The very nature of a *Beyond Your Means* traveler is to spend a great deal of time relaxing and not accomplishing much. There are countless parks, gardens, and other locations throughout the city to truly relax, read, or do some people-watching. When taking a thorough approach, make sure to spend at least an afternoon or evening "relaxing" in a famous place known for its ambiance. Such places to consider are the Luxembourg Gardens or the *Pont des Arts*. When telling others about spending time there, be sure to complete the story by mentioning that you took a lunch consisting of wine, cheese, and bread.

- **Disneyland Paris**: … just kidding.

What Not to Do

There are obviously so many things to do in and around Paris that fitting all of them in is impossible, so you should never feel pressured to do everything. One of the best parts of traveling *Beyond Your Means* is not only discarding the Yankees cap and digital watch but also casting off the preconceived notions of what is really a "must do." Visit what you want and Google the rest.

While there is no reason to feel compelled to say and do all of these suggestions, bear in mind that there are certain things that you should try to avoid completely. In order to develop a list of "what not to do," consider the questions below. Remember, while there is value in doing everything a typical tourist should do, there is also value in avoiding it all.

Would I Do This at Home?

Just as you should ask yourself this question when deciding where to lodge, you should consider it when determining what activities to do. Yes, part of taking a vacation is trying new things—but not if you don't want to. For example, as mentioned previously, there are a lot of cathedrals in Paris, but how many churches have you toured locally? Odds are the answer is "very few" (if any), so there is no reason to feel compelled to visit a nauseating number in Paris.

Also, when considering what to do and what not to do, adding a little more to the question "Would I do this at home?" helps you arrive at an informed answer.

Do I Wish I Could Do This at Home?

While touring Catholic shrines is probably not something you seek out in your hometown, bars where you can spend €30 per drink probably aren't in your daily routine, either. But therein lies the new question. For most people, spending €30 per drink is lunacy, but to many *Beyond Your Means* travelers, this is something that they wish they had the opportunity to do at least weekly in every setting. Therefore, if there is something you wish you could do at home, then move it from the "what not to do" list to the "absolute must" category.

Do Other Travel Guides List It as a "Must-Do"?

An absolute red flag should be raised at full mast for any activity, restaurant, museum, tour, or anything else if it is touted by other travel guides, especially those written by a certain fanny-pack fanatic. The only "must do's" that should ever be considered are those that appear in *Europe Beyond Your Means*. Many vacationers have been stuck at *Paris Plage* during the summer, simply because it is highly recommended in more than one travel guide.

Always ask yourself a few in-depth questions about other travel-guide recommendations. For example, one question that pops to mind is "How good could this really be?" In the case of *Paris Plage*, the banks of the River Seine become a *faux* beach for a few weeks in the summer in an attempt to keep native Parisians happy who can't necessarily afford expensive beach holidays. Themes for *Paris Plage* change annually but generally involve some aspect of French culture. But really, how good could it be? If the theme is French Polynesia, why not just visit French Polynesia? It is difficult to imagine that even the Paris Office of Tourism would argue that a few planted palms and sand on a river compare to Tahiti. While visiting French Polynesia may be impractical, just wait until the theme is the "Culture of the Riviera." When you consider Nice is only ninety minutes via plane or five and a half hours via rail, *Paris Plage* loses most of its luster.

Will This Interfere with My Priorities?

While *Beyond Your Means* travelers may have some difficulty in setting priorities in their domestic lives, generally speaking, their vacation lives are full of rigid ideas. An activity should never be attempted if it would somehow disrupt a more important plan or not go with the theme of the trip. If this is to be the trip where you are a "jet-setter," then is anything gained from the walking tour of Montmartre? Or, if this is the trip where you attempt to convince other travelers that you are working diligently on your novel, then consider the consequences of being spotted on a nighttime mass-market cruise on the Seine by someone who recently heard your outlined plot of a future best-seller at a café. Somehow, enjoying Shirley Temples with Boy Scout Troop 504 from Pasadena takes away from your contrived image.

Again, as with all things *Beyond Your Means*, the most important point is to have fun and fully embrace whatever lifestyle you want. But never feel pressure to take part in something just because it seems like the thing to do. Heed the suggestions for "what to do," but always remember the questions to ask yourself in determining "what not to do." If you don't want to wait in line to see the Eiffel Tower, then don't—and be proud of it. The old elementary school adage "just because everyone else is doing it doesn't mean you should" is a good way to justify not seeing the works of Monet, even if it might actually be a good idea.

The Avant-Garde Approach

It was spring break during one of my years in college and with the euro drastically undervalued, a couple of friends and I decided that it would be a great time to do the whole "London-Paris" thing for nine days. Unfortunately, the group I was with had decided that their method of hanging out in these two mythical cities would be to take on a breakneck pace, scurrying from monuments to museums every day we were there. It didn't take long for me to grow tired of this, since I was sure I'd be there again, and I really didn't want to wake up early most days anyway. Thus, by the time we actually got to Paris, I was in a state of open mutiny with the self-designated group leaders and a punch had been exchanged with a fellow traveler during an alcohol fueled and stressful situation. Needless to say, I was losing popularity quickly.

While this might not have been the most mature attitude to explore the wonders of Paris, I had decided that even though I wouldn't be touring with my companions, I couldn't just sit in bars every day and waste the opportunity. It would have to be sightseeing my way from now on. Most days, I woke up late, missing the complimentary breakfast at the hotel, and headed to a local café to satiate myself. After that, I would walk aimlessly around the city, looking at the various sites and monuments and deciding if the lines out front were short enough to justify my patronage. Being that I got such a late start to the day, many of the most popular places were winding down, which meant I didn't have to spend countless hours in line. One particularly memorable experience was sneaking into the Louvre an hour before closing time. I ignored the "must see" objects that the Louvre is most famous for and instead headed straight for the Italian and Spanish Renaissance paintings section. The relative emptiness of the rooms and the fact that I was basically alone truly allowed me to be moved by the abject beauty of the art. This only lasted for about ten minutes before frantic security guards and large men in black suits came my way instructing me to leave the general area immediately. As it turns out the British Royal family needed to view the collections I had chosen and couldn't be bothered with my presence. Wannabes.

From that point, I really had nothing to do but check my e-mail. It was then that I realized I could rendezvous with a couple of older friends who were experiencing Paris in a different way. These individuals had been around before and were in no mood for restrictive itineraries while on their vacation. For the next three days, we would meet up for dinner, buy bottles of wine at one of the Arab convenience stores, and then tour the most famous monuments at night when they were neither open nor full of tourists. While I did not go inside Notre Dame or climb the Eiffel Tower, I was still struck by their majestic stature and had the time to stand and stare, rather then just checking them off the list before moving onto the next tourist destination.

7

Beyond Paris

It is easy to occupy all of your time in Paris, but to get a better feel for the country, *Beyond Your Means* travelers are encouraged to expand their horizons and take at least a few ventures outside the city in order to differentiate themselves from the unadventurous, boring tourists who rarely leave the capital. To justify side trips, simply ask yourself how many people you know who have ever been to Lyon. Toulouse? Lille? Exactly. By exploring other parts of France, you automatically become the undisputed authority on French travel in your peer group. Undeniably, this is a positive for *Beyond Your Means* travelers who abhor having their sweeping generalizations questioned by others.

Traveling just a few hours outside of the city will provide a multitude of opportunities to splurge on the best wines in the world and sample the authentic cuisines of the French countryside. France is holistically interesting, so it is understandable that the Parisian natives generally spend the month of August outside of their city—but still choose to remain in France.

As a starting point for your trip, consider these tips when planning how to get wherever you are going:

- **The case for cars, too.** Often, travelers forget that simple modern conveniences, such as renting cars, are available in other countries. Everyone knows that traveling through Europe is simple via train, but renting a car will not make travel all that much more arduous. Many travel guides will caution you against renting a car because it is more costly in France than other places, and gas prices in Europe are notoriously high, but do not feel restricted simply because this isn't the norm. Having a car lets you stop and visit anywhere you want, so the cost may be justified by the lack of restrictions.

- **Flights are cheap.** Nations like France are fairly compact when compared to countries in North America, so domestic flights from Paris don't always break the bank. Yes, this is a more expensive way to travel than train or bus (gasp!), but if your destination is Nice, then this shaves a lot of time off of the trip. Flying within a country while on a vacation is unheard of in typical travel lingo, since so much is to be gained while observing the countryside along the way to your destination, but if you honestly couldn't care less, fly.

- **Take the train—but do it the right way**. The preferred method of travel around France is generally accepted to be by rail. *Beyond Your Means* scholars will not refute this point, since you can set your watch by a French rail schedule, and its efficiency is unmatched. But, as with all things, there is one way to do something, and then there is the *Beyond Your Means* way. The French TGV—*train à grande vitesse* (high-speed train)—currently holds the record for the world's fastest train (574.8 km/hour). Thus, no matter what your travel situation, if you can take the TGV to your destination, spend the money and do it. This can be faster than a plane, and there is something to be said for experiencing the best the rails have to offer.

Whether you are taking a TGV or a regular SNCF train, always consider the premiere class ticket. In typical French fashion, train class terms are more blatantly obvious than disguised terms like "business class" and "coach." Instead, the French will come right out and tell you your rank with "first" or "second." Train tickets are one opportunity where spending only 25 to 50 percent more than a second-class passenger will let you call yourself "first class." There are practical reasons for this investment as well, such as the better seating or a meal that is included. There is also a decreased probability of encountering Youth Pass holders asking advice about which "hostile" to stay in next.

With these thoughts in mind, the nation of France—and all of Europe, for that matter—is completely open to you. No matter where you choose to visit during the vacation from your vacation, there are a few cardinal European travel reminders to bear in mind:

- **Pointers on Country Names**. Many visitors to the continent often lack any evidence of having taken high-school social studies, geography, or history. Therefore, remembering a few things about European country names will get you far. For example, it may seem funny, but there is a country named "Georgia" in Eastern Europe. Everyone in Europe knows this, so there is no need to giggle and tell residents of this country how much you enjoyed Atlanta. Also, several countries in Europe have changed names since the publication of many high school textbooks, so remember that Czechoslovakia has been separated into the Czech Republic and Slovakia for quite some time. And finally, while it may be difficult to remember, Austria is a country in Europe, while Australia is a continent in the South Pacific. One had Hapsburgs, while parts of the other have kangaroos.

- **World War II is a sore subject**. No matter where you might be traveling in France, there is no need to discuss the importance of American and British involvement in liberating the nation. Inevitably, this will lead to a debate involving Charles de Gaulle and the "Free French" forces, and everyone will leave unhappy. If traveling in Germany, just avoid the topic altogether.

- **Avoid "Off the Beaten Path" Recommendations**. Basically, if you have read about an off-the-beaten-path destination, that means this particular hotel, restaurant, or site is now very much *on* the beaten path. Travelers should seek out their own hideaway locations instead of taking the highly publicized recommendations of others. It is hard to take any book seriously that recommends off-the-beaten-path locales, yet has a stamp of "Millions sold" or "Now in our tenth printing" on the cover. Furthermore, many times travel writers will have been paid for making such recommendations. Fortunately, the scribes at *Europe Beyond Your Means* have chosen to maintain artistic and creative integrity by avoiding such temptations and suggest that readers find hidden gems on their own. After all, there was a time when Cannes and St. Tropez were off the beaten path, too—ever heard of them?

With these basic ideas in mind, set your sights on the places you would like to visit at your leisure.

Trip Suggestions

Just like traveling within Paris, there are several suggested approaches you can take when looking outside the city for adventures. If you can't figure out where to go, or if a place sounds interesting but you'd rather let someone else do the work, the French government actually employs people whose job it is to tell you where to go on your vacation. These offices are set up in nearly every sizable city in France and are known as *Office de Tourisme* or *Syndicat d'Initiative* (Tourism Office). Finding someone in these offices to offer their opinion on your vacation is about as difficult as going to a Parisian video store and finding a movie staring Gérard Depardieu.

Since there are so many important places to see in France, it is impossible to develop a set list. So, just consider the following categories when planning your trips: 1) Major Cities Other than Paris, 2) Bus Tour Standards, and 3) *La Francophine*.

Major Cities Other than Paris

Contrary to popular belief, France is home to several major cities other than Paris. Most continental Europeans are aware of this fact, but somehow noncontinental tourists manage to avoid the rest of the country's important *villes*. *Europe Beyond Your Means* suggests visiting at least one of the other major French cities to see what life is like outside of Paris. No, do not just visit some small town or what others may refer to as a "village" but a city that plays a role in the French economy.

You are encouraged to at least do a few activities to experience other aspects of French culture in other cities. Below are a few *Beyond Your Means* favorites.

Marseilles

This Mediterranean city is France's second largest and has the third largest metropolitan region. Because of Marseilles' location on the sea and history of shipping, it is a very important city for importing and exporting goods. The central piece to culture and tourism in Marseilles surrounds its opera house, which is one of the most celebrated in Europe. Furthermore, for literary buffs, Marseilles is the setting for the time-honored classic *The Count of Monte Cristo*.

The city is home to multiple museums, such as the *Centre de la Vieille Charité*, with its collections of African and Oceanic art, as well as *Mémorial des Camps de la Mort*, one of the world's most celebrated Holocaust museums.

As far as nightlife is concerned, consider *May Be Blues*, a popular venue for local and international acts, showcasing blues, Cajun, rock 'n' roll, and just about everything else. Or check out the cabaret-style *Le Balthazar*.

When traveling to Marseilles, the TGV from Paris can get you there in about three hours.

Nice

While it is a "nice" place to visit, don't embarrass yourself by pronouncing it that way. This resort town is the *de facto* capital of the *Côte d'Azur* (French Riviera). Staying in Nice is recommended because of its close proximity to Cannes, St. Tropez, and Monte Carlo, and there is no reason to miss out on saying, "Oh, I've been there."

Nice's history as a resort town is evident by the Roman bathhouse ruins. And no French city is without art, so a tourist might want to check out the Henri Matisse Museum. Additionally, Nice has everything that a touristy resort town near the beach should have. Along the *Promenade des Anglais*, visitors get a glimpse to the closest version of Venice Beach that the French are willing to offer. Rollerbladers glide by drink stands, while sunbathing tourists lounge in the blue chairs dotting the coast. The best tip for a foreign tourist along the beach is to not appear surprised or grab your camera when encountering topless female sunbathers or snickering too obviously at the European male's embrace of the Speedo.

Nightlife in Nice is full of clubs and bars along the *Promenade des Anglais*, as well as in the *Vieux Nice* area. The most popular nightlife spot in Nice for *Beyond Your Means* travelers is *Chez Wayne's*, which is quite reminiscent of any rowdy spring-break destination. Basically, you will be flashed and offered shots. Also, *Thor Pub* is a popular destination, offering the traditional ladies nights and generous happy-hour specials, complete with Viking battle axes and wood shields on the walls. Since Nice is located so close to other towns, checking out the Monte Carlo or Cannes nightlife is certainly doable.

Nice offers plenty of elite resorts, such as *Hotel Palais Masterlinck* with its nine acres of gardens along the sea; *Hotel Negresso*, decorated with Salvador Dali paintings; and *Palais de la Mediterranee* with its stunning gaming room. But as a resort town, cheap lodging is also plentiful, including an Ibis hotel that is only about one block from the train station, as well as a multitude of small, two-star family-run hotels, located right in *Veux Nice*, three blocks from the beach.

Convenient flights operate between Nice and Paris' Orly Airport quite frequently. Also, even France now has a low-cost rail carrier, the IdTGV train, which is very economical and has direct service to Nice from Paris. *Europe Beyond Your Means* doesn't feel comfortable recommending any low-cost carrier, be it air or rail, but will not discourage its use.

Lyon

The third largest city in France with the second largest metropolitan region, Lyon is located in the eastern part of the country. Historically, Lyon has been recognized in many circles as the culinary capital of France, and knowing this factoid will help you sound more informed than those who just assume that title is bestowed on Paris. Lyon is also an architecture aficionado's dream because it is home to some of the best Renaissance-style structures in the world. Moreover, Lyon is an exceptional "on the way" stopover, as it can be reached *en route* from Paris to the Mediterranean beaches or the Alps.

Lyon is home to the second largest number of haute-cuisine restaurants in France; obviously, Paris has the most. *Paul Bocuse* is considered by many to be the best restaurant in Lyon and sports a five-star rating. The restaurant's namesake established himself as one of the most famous and public chefs of the twentieth century. The original restaurant is located just north of the city, but in Lyon, Paul Bocuse also operates *Le Nord*, *l'Est*, *Le Sud* and *l'Ouest*, each of which is focused on a different type of French cuisine. Cheaper than the original, they still allow *Beyond Your Means* travelers to drop the name "Bocuse" when later discussing their evening meals, but then again, so can visitors to EPCOT Center. While dining at any of Lyon's restaurants, be sure to have a glass or two of *Côtes du Rhône* or *Beaujolais*, since these are two of the staples that originated in the area.

As with any major city, the nightlife in Lyon can still be considered diverse and bustling but less subject to change than Paris. At night, more than one hundred of its architectural spots are illuminated, making for a great stroll through the city. The club scene features many notable selections, such as *Koubalibre,* which fills the role of a one-stop shop for entertainment. This club is a restaurant, discotheque, and karaoke bar, and the various offerings speak to the eclectic crowd it attracts. Also, the English-style bar *Albion* is worth a visit. *Albion* features two giant screens for concerts and sporting events, a dartboard, and a wide selection of draught beers, and hosts concerts on Wednesdays. You can also try to turn a quick buck—or euro, that is—to fund the rest of your vacation in Lyon's casino, *Le Lyon Vert.*

If you happen to win big on red 27, then instead of getting ahead on your car payments, consider upgrading your lodging to the *Cour des Loges* or *Villa Florentine.* Otherwise, Lyon has plenty of small hotels to accommodate the *Europe Beyond Your Means* standard of travel style and class.

Getting to Lyon is very simple, since there are numerous daily flights from Paris. Additionally, Lyon was the first ever TGV destination, so this has proven a popular route.

Strasbourg

The French just absolutely love Strasbourg because, as the capital of Alsace, it has changed hands with the Germans multiple times during various wars and, by God, France now has it! Naturally, much of Strasbourg's architecture and cuisine is heavily influenced by Germany, due to history and close proximity. Strasbourg's international flare is supported by being the center for the European Court of Human Rights; the headquarters of the European military force, Eurocorps; the main campus of France's national training school for civil servants (*L'École nationale d'administration*); and a meeting place for the European Parliament.

Besides touring all of the important international sites in the city, Strasbourg is also home to several impressive museums, such as *Musée d'Art Moderne et Contemporain,* museum of modern and contemporary art, which houses works by Degas, Rodin, and many others. Also, the park of the *Orangerie* is a rather interesting place to spend a few hours enjoying the natural splendor of the region, with its waterfall, lake, and zoo. For a look at the heavily German-influenced section, take a tour of *Place de la République.*

Strasbourg nightlife is rather vibrant, as there are a lot of students craving fun and a lot of diplomats who are eager to spend tax dollars. The *La Petite France* district is a great starting point for a night out, with its many restaurants, bars, and clubs. Specifically, *Le Seven* dance club attracts the beautiful crowd, and *L'Exils* is notable for its casual dartboard/pinball atmosphere.

Traveling via TGV to Strasbourg has proven very popular since the service recently opened. But flights from Paris are very quick and generally very cheap, if booked in advance.

France has many other important cities that are worth a visit, so do not limit yourself to these recommendations. Think about also visiting Toulouse, Bordeaux, Nantes, Angers, Lille, or any number of others. No matter where you choose, remember the importance of visiting at least one other major city, as that will make you seem like more of an authority on the country than those who limit their stays exclusively to Paris.

Bus Tour Standards

Much like highlights within the city of Paris, sometimes the cookie-cutter tours get it right. There are countless attractions around France that are worth your while, but inevitably, all tour companies offer a few basic options that even *Beyond Your Means* travelers should consider. This is an excellent opportunity to utilize the local tourism offices. If you want to see Christmas come early for someone, ask a French staff member for information and their opinions on anything. Yes, at these spots you will be joining the "are we there yet?" crowd, but grin and bear it while checking off a few essentials. For each of these excursions, there are numerous tour operators and buses leaving Paris daily.

Loire Valley

Every *Beyond Your Means* traveler enjoys the work of those who epitomize a decadent lifestyle, and the many chateaux in the Loire Valley give something to daydream about. For hundreds of years, the French royal court was held at various castles in the Loire Valley. It seems that each ruler tried to outdo his predecessors by building a more impressive residence, thus illustrating that the Sun King was not the first pretentious ruler of the nation. The most famous chateaux include *Châteaux d'Amboise*, **Château de Villandry** and **Chenonceau**. Also, the beautiful countryside alone provides a peaceful retreat from the pressures of big-city life. And, as with basically everywhere in France, the region has its own unique wines for all to sample. Thus, it is easy to see why the Loire Valley is a popular weekend retreat for many Parisians.

Mont St. Michel

This location is one of the most toured in France. The land area is sometimes an island and sometimes not, due to the various tidal periods. It is situated just off the coast of Normandy, was originally a monastery, and played an important role in William the Conqueror's Norman Conquest. For a brief period in the 1800s, it was converted to a prison, then closed a few years later. In recent years it has been used as a monastery again.

Champagne Region

For "sparking wine" to be classified as "champagne," it must come from this particular region in France. On the way to the heart of the Champagne region, check out the cathedral in Reims, which served as the coronation site of French kings for centuries. Note that the anointing oil that was used for coronation is still housed at the cathedral, in case the French ever decide to switch back to a monarchy. Starting from Epernay at the *Moët & Chandon* headquarters or the *Dom Pérignon* vineyards is probably the easiest and most comprehensive tour in the region. While the temptation exists to buy lots of emblematic material in the *Moët & Chandon* gift shop, remember they are famous for champagne, not salt and pepper shakers. Nearly every champagne house in the region offers tours, so feel free to supplement your favorite champagne instead of *Moët & Chandon*; just be wise enough to call ahead to find out if they are offering a tour on your intended day of travel.

The Beaches of Normandy

The beaches and cemeteries along the Normandy coast will humble even the most ostentatious *Beyond Your Means* travelers. Take the time to visit this location, as it is the spot where the course of the world's future was determined. Staying at the little town of Caen will also give you a chance to visit the castle of William the Conqueror. Guided tours of the battlefields and beaches can be arranged at the *Mémorial pour la Paix* (Peace Museum), which is just north of downtown and easily accessible by the city's public transport.

Wine Tours

Taking a tour of wine country isn't really possible, since practically the entire nation is "wine country"—it just depends on which kind of wine you are looking for. As mentioned, the Loire Valley is an excellent region for wine, as are Alsace, Bordeaux, Burgundy, Champagne, Languedoc-Roussillon, and the Rhône Valley, just to name a few. Ideally, you can dovetail your wine tour with other adventures, but be sure to take at least one tour and splurge on a few bottles that you cannot buy at home.

Where to Be and When

Within the nation of France, several interesting events are held that you may want to plan trips around. Think about these events before settling on plans:

February

- Nice Carnival. Often known by its other name, Mardi Gras, this is a two-week-long street party in Nice, known for the elegance and multitude of its flowers and perpetual nightlife. The Nice Carnival almost always falls sometime in February, as it is scheduled to be the day before Ash Wednesday. But it can sometimes start as late as March 9. Most tourists aren't in France during the dead of the winter, so if you find yourself there, consider taking the trip down to Nice to be part of the action.

May

- Cannes Film Festival. A private festival held annually (usually in the month of May) at the *Palais des Festivals et des Congrès* in the resort town of Cannes. There is nothing but *Beyond Your Means* travel opportunities in Cannes, so much so that it is advised to stay elsewhere and just travel into Cannes during the day and evening to be a part of the pompous and highfalutin celebrations. Unless you're able to commandeer a bed on someone's yacht, Cannes is extremely expensive and humbling. Staying outside of Cannes—in Nice, for instance—is a good idea. It's a quick and easy train ride, plus it may actually save you enough money to buy a drink while in Cannes and look like you actually belong there.

- Garcon du Café Race. This is an entertaining race run by café waiters, carrying drinks on their trays, through the streets of Paris, scheduled in late May. If you think waiters in Paris don't hustle enough for your liking, this event might change your mind.

- The French Open. The competition begins at Roland Garros Stadium in late May and goes forward into June. This event is part of tennis' Grand Slam and is a bit flashier and literally more colorful than the infamous lawn tennis club across the Channel.

June

- Paris Jazz Festival. The dates vary from year to year, but it usually starts sometime in June. Jazz is an authentic American invention, but between the two world wars, a small community of African-American jazz musicians moved to France to escape segregation. This created an expatriate musical scene and formally introduced jazz to the French. Often called the "Harlem Renaissance in Montmartre," these artists contributed to a culture that thrived for two decades, until the occupation of the city by German forces in 1940. Thus, Paris has an established jazz culture in its own right, influenced by but distinct from America's.

- Le Mans Race. This twenty-four-hour car race is held in the tiny town of Le Mans, typically in June but subject to change. Because of the time requirement, the race is known as the Grand Prix of Endurance.

July

- Tour de France. Any stage of this twenty-day-plus race can be exciting. It always concludes near the very end of July, with several laps around Paris. Standing along the *rue de Rivoli* or the *Champs-Élysées* drinking champagne while cheering on the participants is *Beyond Your Means* sporting at its best.

- Quatorze Juillet (Fourteenth of July or Bastille Day). The French version of the Fourth of July, except instead of commemorating the defeat of an oppressor, it commemorates storming a jail in Paris and letting all the prisoners out. It celebrates the first act that eventually led to the current "republic" that France is today. Much like national celebrations in other countries, you can expect to see the Tricolor everywhere, crowded streets, and pyrotechnic pageantry.

November

- Armistice Day (November 11). Ceremonies at the *Arc de Triomphe* include a military parade down the Champs-Élysées. This is the day the French president lays a wreath on the Tomb of the Unknown Solider in front of the eternal flame. This flame is intended to be eternal—except for the time the drunk Mexican chose to make it "ephemeral."

- Beaujolais Nouveau Day. The day in all of France where the release of a brand-new mediocre Beaujolais wine is celebrated like a national holiday. French law sets this as the third Thursday in November each year. Officially "released" at midnight on Thursday morning (or Wednesday night, depending on how you look at it).

La Francophonie

Thanks to imperialism and narcissism, the French have left a stamp on the world, from Canada to the South Pacific. While spending time in France, you may want to expand your horizons a bit by visiting places outside of the country where a strong French influence persists. While venturing to Tahiti may be a bit extreme—though, of course, not discouraged—there are several places for you to consider vacationing for a few days or a week to experience an exported French culture.

For starters, French culture is found to some degree all over Europe, especially in countries bordering France. Taking a few days to visit Francophone regions of Belgium, Switzerland, and Luxembourg will allow you to check a few more countries off your list, while also seeing the sites these places have to offer. (As a cautionary point, before visiting these countries, please check your local bookstore for additional editions of *Europe Beyond Your Means*. Not to give any secrets away, but *Europe Beyond Your Means: The Wallonia Tour* will rival *Gone With the Wind*.)

The French sphere of influence is quite large; thus, side trips outside of metropolitan France could be very exciting and exotic. Provided the flight or train ride isn't too long and doesn't take you too far from your temporary Parisian home (or too close to your actual home), give the far reaches of the former empire a whirl. Consider that France maintains very strong ties with its former African colonies, and flights from Paris to North African cities have proven to be fairly reasonable in price and time. Casablanca may no longer have the romantic draw inspired by Humphrey Bogart and Ingrid Bergman, and the streets certainly aren't safe, but at least you'll get to hear "Frarabic."

The Big Gamble

After months of mental preparation, I finally had the opportunity to head to Monte Carlo to toss a few dice and conceal a few cards with the truly rich and famous. I've gambled everywhere from Las Vegas to Indian casinos in Connecticut and North Carolina to some of the most dingy locations in Tunica, Mississippi. If gambling has a hierarchy, Monte Carlo is clearly perched at the top, and it was finally my turn to participate.

The mystique surrounding Monte Carlo's casino was enough to draw me from the United States, let alone Paris. Generally, I have no problem encountering new situations or embarking on the unfamiliar, but at the very least, I always have some idea of what to expect. In this case, I had only lore as a guide.

I stayed at a relatively inexpensive hotel in Nice the night before, in order to conserve a few centimes before heading out for my "Casino Royale" day. While preparing for the trip, my biggest concern was dress code. All I knew was that in literature and film, everyone in the casino donned the best evening wear money could buy. The questions presented themselves: Should I take a tuxedo? If so, would the others be able to tell that it wasn't custom tailored by a famous designer? What if they all were wearing white jackets and I was in black? Or vice versa? And on and on. Ultimately, I determined to visit the casino during the day, as the dress code was more predictable, and I was less likely to be noticeably out-priced at every table. Eventually, I considered all factors: It is summer. It is hot. I am young. I am not famous. I want an air of mystery. I don't want to stand out. After pondering for longer than I should have, I chose a light-colored Belgian linen Brooks Brothers suit, a light-blue dress shirt, no tie, and well-placed designer sunglasses.

After exiting the train and taking a taxi directly to the casino, I quickly noticed there were countless tourists outside the structure snapping photographs of the building, while only a couple people seemed to actually be going inside. I got out of the taxi, paid, and then noticed that two men were standing outside the doors with what appeared to be clipboards with lists on them.

Lists? I hadn't anticipated this. Could it be that the casino was not a public facility? Of course this was possible; why would I think otherwise? Quickly, before anyone noticed that I was standing, craving instruction, I began to walk to the obviously public café at the side of the building.

I ordered a café au lait and began to sip it as slowly as possible, taking note of people entering the building. Did they look like they belonged? Did they look "public" enough for me to think I could go in? Were those two men really looking at lists of people who could enter? When there was absolutely no trace of liquid in my cup, I decided it was time to get a better look. I took a stroll toward the building to see what was happening. In the distance, I saw Grimaldi Castle, where the true royalty were looking over their wealthy principality.

When I arrived, I tried to gather as much confidence as possible to ascend the long staircase to the entrance, bypass the potential gatekeepers, and wait for them to ask for my name. But again, I lost all gumption at the thought of having to descend the stairs, defeated, in front of numerous onlookers. To add another level to my anxiety, there was a sign that obviously gave instructions, but I had forgone my prescription glasses for the designer sunglasses and couldn't read it. I made the quick decision to bypass the stairs and began walking around the edges of the building, where many others were also looking at the beautiful harbor.

Finally, I decided it was now or never. I had come all this way with one goal, and I needed to try. I looked the part, so it was time to act the part. I went back around to the front of casino, began my ascension up the stairs, careful to not be so quick as to draw attention. There were a few others walking up the stairs the same time as I. I got to the doorway, and the two men standing there, who I thought held my fate in their hands, simply offered "Bonjour, monsieur." Thank God! Apparently, whatever they were holding did not contain a list of those allowed to enter this storied establishment.

There was a slight line to pay the nominal daily cover fee of €10. At this point, I began to be a little disappointed. Those in line in front of me had obviously taken less time in planning appropriate attire than I had. T-shirts and jeans hardly seemed correct, but I was in the minority. Once entering the actual gaming room, it became apparent that within the Monte Carlo casino existed a clear social divide, with certain individuals being relegated to the rooms in the front and others being whisked away to private rooms, yet many of us shared the same bar.

While standing beside poorly clothed tourists making minimal bets, I watched groups of individuals, wearing suits that cost more than my car, walking into rooms, where the doors were then locked. In the back of my mind, I realized that exclaiming "Baby needs a new pair of shoes" wouldn't be inappropriate at my table; thus, my disappointment grew. Every now and then, the private games would obviously take a break and the high-rollers would gather for a drink at the bar near us plebeians. I quickly determined that the place to be was by the bar.

I spent the better part of an hour eavesdropping and slipping cigarettes out of my authentic-looking "silver" cigarette case. I considered it a victory when the occasional private-room gambler would offer a "bonjour," "bonjourno," or even "hello." To my side, throughout this time, were two rather elegant-looking young blondes, casually sipping away at champagne. I wondered to myself if they came with a prix fixe cost.

Eventually, this experience grew old, so I decided my time at the Monte Carlo casino should end. I didn't want to be seen playing slots and couldn't enter that night's €100,000 buy-in tournament. I strolled out of the building, happy to have attended, but disappointed that I hadn't been part of the real event. I took a bit of pride in knowing that I was part of at least two or three tourist photographs of the entrance, but I vowed to return someday, when I, too, could be part of the mystery that existed in the private rooms.

8

Avoiding Les Faux Pas

In order to have a complete *Beyond Your Means* experience, preparing beforehand to conduct yourself in a manner acceptable to the natives and believable to the other tourists is vital. For example, buying a beret with your initials embroidered on it before embarking on the trip is a purchase that should be avoided. Pay careful attention to the advice contained within the next two chapters to avoid certain *faux pas* while in a city known for its exclusivity.

Faux French Stereotypes

For the most part, Europeans—and specifically, the French—are just like every other civilized Western society. Sure, the French pretentiously sip champagne whenever it pleases them, use the most dismissive conversational shrug on the planet, and shamelessly parade topless on their beaches, but we love them all the more for it. The fact is that a large number of negative French characterizations hearken back to a post-war era long since passed.

When traveling to Paris, it is important to abandon strongly held stereotypes of the city and the people and certainly not comment on them to the French. Just think: it doesn't take Dale Carnegie to point out that no matter where you are in the world, saying "So I hear you people are rude" isn't going to "win friends and influence people."

"It's Like a Forest under There"

After deciding to go to France and informing your friends, there will be the inevitable locker-room banter regarding French women. Yes, the French are well known for having an ample supply of classic beauties, who will offer no more than a smirk on the street. But within a few minutes of discussing the merits of Gallic ladies, the conversation often leads to an archaic and flawed conventional wisdom regarding their daily beauty rituals.

Everyone has that friend—the one who always interjects the same vapid comments about European women when you tell him you're dating one, met one on a recent holiday, or just engaged in a dalliance with one during a recent bender in the 5th. The comments usually progress in a highbrow and sophisticated manner, culminating in the unavoidable "Dude, she's European. She doesn't shave her armpits, does she?"

On the all-important armpit issue, this stereotype is categorically not true. Perhaps at one time, French women did not shave under their arms, but shaving began in France shortly after it did in the United States. As a matter of fact, underarm forests are much more common in Berkeley, California, than on the typical street in Paris. Rest assured, there will be no unpleasant surprises when *Sophie* or *Monique* is hailing a cab or raising her arms to show just how "sure" she is, too.

As devoid of fact and intellect as the statements regarding female grooming habits are, they still serve as the perfect framework for our point of avoiding outdated stereotypes.

"You Know the French Don't Bathe"

Paramount to all French stereotypes is the supposed lack of hygiene. The English are constantly purporting that the French finish dead last in some dubiously sponsored EU survey on hygiene year after year. This survey, however, continues to remain elusive to our *Beyond Your Means* research analysts. We therefore doubt its authenticity. On the other hand, if the French really are the last nation in Europe to utilize the *bain,* at least one can argue they are the only nation to do something about it. After all, perfume wasn't perfected in Amsterdam.

Whatever your position is on Gallic hygiene, there is still the little matter of the Turkish toilet—an awkward first introduction, to say the least. For readers not familiar with the general concept, a Turkish toilet is a toilet used by squatting, not sitting, over a hole in the ground. While the French may not accept the idea of Turkey's being European for cultural issues, they were more than willing to adopt this cultural quirk. Many a tourist returns from Paris indignant about the two white footprints on the floor where the bowl and seat should be. However, like all things French, there is a viewpoint that changes what seems like utter incivility into progressiveness. For instance, Turkish toilets are actually considered to be more anatomically correct, so perhaps the French are on to something. Therefore, there is no need to run from café to café in search of more respectable, should one say, modern facilities. There is a trend currently in the United States to abandon the "porcelain God" in favor a method that provides a more efficient method of personal waste disposal. However, until that movement becomes commonplace on all sides of the pond, an American tourist should think of the Turkish toilet as a naturalist experience. In some ways, France can be like camping—in a really expensive department store full of material objects, great wine, and sophistication, with an end result of enlightenment instead of taxidermy.

Due to a few overheard conversations, included in the thoughts regarding hygiene is advice that shouldn't be necessary but, sadly, is. Remember that France is part of Western Europe. So inoculations are not required before visiting, and the water is absolutely fine. *Pierre* does not take revenge in the harsh manner that Montezuma does.

"Paris Is Just So Dirty"

Another troublesome stereotype is that Paris is a particularly dirty city. This stems from so many tourists visiting who have not been to many major cities and are appalled at any trash on the streets. Paris is no dirtier than any other major city, and it spends excessively more than most places on street cleaning.

"The French Are Just So Rude"

Well, it isn't necessarily false that the French are rude, but this can be explained a bit. The French, Parisians especially, are markedly more rude than the average resident of Charlotte but not too many standard deviations above residents of other truly major cities.

New Yorkers are just as infamous for lacking a "howdy y'all" attitude; Londoners would rather read the *Financial Times* than greet strangers on the street; and natives of Tokyo will shove and push you around like a first-time chopstick-user with rice. While the French might saunter dismissively through their capital more than most cultures, the burdens of big-city life are still omnipresent. The fact of the matter is that Paris is a major metropolitan city, where people have stressful jobs and places to be five minutes ago. Therefore, one should expect the same urban attitude found everywhere else in the world. Parisians aren't as rude as they are misunderstood, and perhaps the best way to describe them isn't necessarily as rude but, instead, as focused on themselves.

The best advice we offer in dealing with Parisians is to take time to be friendly, attempt a little French, and try not to waste too many people's time.

"The French Hate All Americans"

This belief is quite strongly held by many people, but the fact is that the French do not hate all Americans; they hate all American politicians. Well, that isn't exactly true, either. Really, though, the French do not necessarily hold Americans with a higher disregard than they do anyone else who isn't privileged enough to be French. But the unique attitude toward Yanks is worthy of mention. Franco-American relations have been odd, at best, for hundreds of years because the two nations are so interconnected, much like two college roommates who have spent too much time together.

Both sides can thank the other for freedom and important contributions to their cultures. France has given the United States gastronomy, classical music, and priceless art, while the United States has returned the favor to France in the form of rock 'n' roll and cheese fries. The French are vitriolic defenders of their language and culture and grow a bit squeamish anytime they aren't the world hegemon. The bottom line is that both the United States and France feel their particular brand of social justice would better benefit the world as a whole.

Furthermore, both the French and the Americans are forced to deal with one another constantly, because of high rates of tourism and the fact that neither country is ever willing to be silent on world affairs. It is no secret that France and the United States often take opposite opinions on many hot-button political issues, so many French do despise American politicians. Sometimes this translates into a peculiar attitude toward all Americans, especially those who eat "freedom fries."

Vrai French Stereotypes

While many beliefs about the French are misinformed and outdated, some commonly held thoughts are as true as saying that Texans like their barbeque. Become familiar with these as soon as possible, so as to not act surprised when confronted with the reality firsthand.

The French Love Dogs, and Everything about Them

There are dogs everywhere in Paris—everywhere. The French love dogs as much as they do rioting. If it is to be accepted that the French people aren't categorically any ruder than their other urban counterparts, their dogs should still be noted for their heightened boorishness. Getting the opportunity to pet a French dog is all but impossible, given the sense of superiority possessed by these entitled four-legged creatures. An American dog is excitable, ready to fetch and play with strangers, while a French dog is aloof and more ready for a "pet-icure."

Also, sometimes shocking to tourists is the readiness of the French to ignore the puppy excrement that perpetually appears on the streets. In other cities around the world, laws exist requiring pet owners to be responsible for the accidents and necessities of man's best friend. Such laws do not exist in Paris; instead the French have another system.

Since a Frenchmen cannot be expected to bend over and handle the former contents of an animal, the government uses taxpayer money for a *flotte* of motorbikes armed with a vacuum to suck up these steaming piles of inconvenience. If you ever encounter a seemingly normal looking motorcycle on the street that has a profound smell, more likely than not this is an individual with the illustrious job title of *motto-crotteur*, paid by the government to free the streets of dog *crotte*.

The French Avoid Working

Perhaps this is their most endearing quality of all. The French sacrifice a great deal, including their economy, for the sake of *joie de vivre*. Especially in the unlikely event that your *Beyond Your Means* adventure is somehow work-related, knowing about the French approach to *travail* is important.

In addition to the government-guaranteed five weeks of vacation per year, the French are quite proud of their "JRTT," *jour de recuperation de temps du travail*. This is the one day each month that employers allow employees to rest and relax instead of working. Additionally, a French prime minister recently stated that he is investigating the idea of corporate naptime, because roughly one-third of the French have sleeping issues and *un petit do-do* would increase productivity. Needless to say, this trend has yet to reach Wall Street or Canary Wharf.

Love Is Everywhere

Paris is the city of romance, and French is the language *d'amour*; therefore, a traveler is likely to see obnoxious examples of love on every corner. European attitudes, in general, are much more accepting of public displays of affection. Consequently, it may be necessary to keep a close eye when walking down the street or across a bridge to avoid the countless couples engaged only in one another. On any given day, a *Beyond Your Means* traveler can attempt to top the previous day's number of couples seen kissing in public places.

Always remember that public displays of affection that lack restraint aren't necessarily exemplified by locals. Oftentimes, this showcase is provided by the numerous foreign couples who think it is more acceptable to be seen engaged in public foreplay just because they are in Paris. The French are willing to embrace one another just about anywhere, but so is everyone else in Paris. Because of the love culture, France is highly recommended as a romantic getaway as well as a *Beyond Your Means* destination, but bear in mind that you will not be the first person to make reference to "French kissing."

Not Becoming a Stereotype Yourself

France is inundated with tourists, both *Beyond Your Means* and within-your-means folks alike, especially in the summer months, so it is easy to understand why the French have developed harsh opinions of those who visit their country. Stopping a bus driver in the 4th to ask, in English, where a no-name hotel is located would be just one example of living up to their preconceived notions. The best way to avoid becoming just another tourist is to carefully consider your actions in all circumstances. This advice goes beyond instructing you that the only travel guide you should open on the street is *Europe Beyond Your Means*.

Moreover, when plotting your next move, consider your actions as a reflection on your own culture. Also, try to put yourself in a Parisian's shoes. Ricknicks might think it's acceptable to pester a waiter during the lunch hour by asking him the quickest way to the *Musée d'Orsay* or what exhibits he recommends, but *Beyond Your Means* travelers know better. Lunch hour in a café is not the time to attempt pleasantries with a man who makes his whole living careening from table to table. *Beyond Your Means* travelers may not be workers in their own right, but they at least recognize and respect the institution.

The tired, worn-out humor used by European visitors has made natives rather callous in conversation with people who are obviously tourists. For example, any Brit can describe the annoyance they experience all summer long by the number of witty individuals who think they're the very first person on the planet to mimic the automated conductor's voice on the London Tube—"Mind the gap. Mind the gap." France also has its own share of exhausted jokes. Avoiding linguistic embarrassments is very important, so readers must remember to never say anything trite. Think of the following illustration as an example:

A few American funny-guys, recent college graduates, are on their last free-for-all before starting "real life." During their travels, they decide to hit up the local café after a rough night at the 3-Ducks "Hostile." They drank at the "hostile's" bar until late; then got tossed out relatively early in the morning. They're not feeling marathon quality or even polite, considering the circumstances. They have no choice but to accept their situation, so salvaging breakfast is really the only option before they head to Amsterdam on a quest for the finest menu selection of ganja, not the Anne Frank museum. They settle on a nearby and empty café in the 15th. Their waiter, *François*, approaches the de facto leader known as American Funny Guy, who then unsubtly sounds "ribit, ribit" with each step *François* makes toward their table. *François* ignores the brilliance of their insult and asks them, in English, what they'd like to eat. American Funny Guy decides that this would be a great time to ask for "French toast." *François* appears confused at first, but then understands the attempted slight because of the covert "low fives" being exchanged at the table. *François* informs American Funny Guy that they don't have French toast.

However, this is what American Funny Guy wanted to hear, so he continues on: "Are you sure? We are in France. You must have some French toast back there." His hung-over comrades' giggle escalates to a guffaw, as American Funny Guy nods the bill of his baseball cap toward the kitchen without looking at François.

François endures. "*Non*, we don't have *zee* French toast, *monsieur*. Would you like *zomezing* else?"

"Well, OK, then. If you don't have French toast, then I guess I'll have French fries and scrambled eggs." His friends are close to a comedic orgasm and can barely get out their orders. When they eventually finish their meal, they call the waiter over with an arrogant gesture and using the outdated title "*Garçon!*" Needless to say, they did not graduate from a particularly impressive university.

Thematically, it's neither cute nor funny to ask a waiter for French fries, French toast, or French dressing. Asking for all three together, with intended simultaneous use, might be funny, as that could potentially be the first time anyone every requested them collectively, but for the most part, you should avoid the clichés. Basically, if you're thinking of just filling the air with the same old tired *merde*, reconsider. If travel companions persist in this exercise, you may want to consider public castigation and harsh ridicule to teach them a lesson and regain some credibility with the French.

The Recurring Litmus Test: Would I Do This at Home?

This point cannot be stressed enough; if you wouldn't do something or perform a particular set of actions at home, you should probably skip them while abroad as well. This could potentially be anything, but suffice it to say, *Europe Beyond Your Means* is not trying to regulate or quell socially *avant-garde* behavior as much as guide practitioners away from poor choices. You wouldn't consider sleeping outside New York's Penn Station, so why would you think it is any less risky or acceptable at *Gare du Nord*? No matter what, keep this advice in mind at all times.

What to Expect

Evolving from the ideas of "what to do" and "what not to do" is "what to expect." Preparing yourself for certain differences is important, since Paris is in a foreign country and therefore, every aspect of day-to-day life won't be exactly the same. So many differences are not logical but can simply be justified by saying, "It's France."

The French do things slightly different than you might in your own country. Some of their ideas are antiquated, some of them are actually better, and some of them are different just to be different because they're French. For instance, expect to pay more for Coke or Fanta than you would for a cheap bottle of wine. It might not make sense, but "It's France." Besides, a bottle of Viognier in the spring is sportier than a can of Coke any day. Regardless of your opinion on any matter, making continuous comments on the "right way to do things" is probably best left to those like American Funny Guy, unless you want to be disliked everywhere you go and have their departures celebrated only after you're already gone.

Not unlike American Funny Guy, another popular anti-hero, possibly American Funny Guy's dad, will serve to further illustrate this advice: it's "Executive Track Guy." This omnipresent fellow is currently halfway up the management pipeline at GE and knows everything there is to know about efficiency and product quality. He never leaves home without an updated edition of *Six Sigma* or *Leading Change*. He is aroused by using a spreadsheet to calculate the price per ounce of his favorite beers, playing golf with his bosses on Saturday mornings, and lying together in sexual congress with "Mrs. Executive Track Guy" every Wednesday precisely at 9:15. Executive Track Guy has just finished lecturing the waiter at an upscale *brasserie* on the relative merits and potential customer satisfaction if the restaurant would put a little ice in his glass of Coke and offer free refills. His smug satisfaction comes from feeling he is on a mission to set the world right. He holds his head high with a protruding chest, as he drags Mrs. Executive Track Guy along across the street. Just then he spots a *tabac* and wonders exactly what the French are doing with these stores he sees everywhere. He has decided that he'll go in and have a peek around to discover what else he can fix in this backwards city.

When he enters the store, he spots a cabinet full of cigars behind the counter. He thinks quickly how cool and sophisticated he can appear at the next golf outing, passing around Cuban cigars to upper management. He snaps at a gentleman behind the counter, *Arnaud,* who is in the middle of assisting an elderly woman with the purchase of a *carte orange.* "Hey, you guys got any Cuban cigars?" he asks, framed more like a suspicious interrogation rather than an actual inquiry. *Arnaud* responds, after finishing up with the elderly woman, "Of course, monsieur, we have all kinds." Notable is that Executive Track Guy doesn't know that outside of the United States, Cuban cigars are the natural swizzle sticks of choice. You can find other kinds of cigars but, by and large, the majority on the market are exports of Cuba. *Arnaud* knows that Executive Tack Guy doesn't know this, and he also knows that Executive Track Guy has only heard of a Cuban cigar with the brand name "Cohiba." *Arnaud* asks Executive Track Guy what kind of cigar he'd like, and he responds, "Just give me twelve of your best Cohibas."

Arnaud asks, "What size would you like?" Executive Track Guy says, "The typical size; what do you think? And make sure they're the best ones, or

I'll just go somewhere else and get a better price." It would behoove Executive Track Guy to realize that tobacco is regulated by the French government. Cigars are the same price all over the country, and the quality standards are typically better than world average in every Parisian *tabac*. It would have also helped for him to understand that "Cohiba" is a brand name used, in both Cuba and the Dominican Republic, by entirely different companies.

Arnaud is tired of Executive Track Guy. He goes to the humidor and pulls out twelve Dominican-made Cohibas in a petite corona size, a cigar type most commonly used after breakfast rather than on the golf course. Executive Track Guy deviantly pays for his prize as he ponders the social cachet the cigars will bring him later. *Arnaud* smiles as Executive Track Guy drags his silent wife back out of the store. Not only did Executive Track Guy not get "Cubans," he was privately emasculated as well. Not for nothing, Arnaud won the day.

With everything that seems different in Paris, the best advice is to accept ignorance on certain subjects and approach everything with an open mind and curious attitude. The French are more than willing to educate travelers on the proper way to conduct themselves, so simply ask questions that will lead to answers that you do not know.

Relating to Those Back Home

Conduct in Paris is the most important section of this chapter, but a *Beyond Your Means* traveler should never neglect those back home. These are the individuals who have nurtured and supported, yet privately criticized, you for embarking on such a trip. Finding ways to keep in touch with them, especially if they have helped finance the trip, is a gesture that, unfortunately, Emily Post and Amy Vanderbilt neglected to describe.

Taking steps to remember those unfortunately left behind will prove greatly beneficial when planning *Beyond Your Means* adventures in the future. Thanks to modern technology, many individuals often take the liberty of placing their large photo albums online and e-mailing links titled "Bob's trip to France." Quite creatively, these albums often include photos titled "Bob at the Eiffel Tower," "Debauchery," "One Night in Paris," or other such original designations. However, e-mails with links to these albums can often annoy the folks who are diligently working their nine-to-fives. While they may find some element of humor in pictures of you with a Styrofoam *Arc de Triomphe* on your head, remember that there is no need to ever make them jealous or let them have visual evidence that you are not in Paris for exclusively cultural purposes.

Keeping in touch with those on the home front is crucial as well. In the age of mass communication, there is truly no need to send a postcard to friends unless they really, really want it. Some people might want an item with a foreign postage stamp, but most simply do not care. To keep in touch nowadays, e-mail works best. Perhaps to add some cultural flair, instead of closing the e-mail with the standard "Sincerely" or "Best," try "*Au revoir.*" Your friends at home will treasure it forever.

Paris is unquestionably the most storied shopping city in the world, and this fact should be treated with respect when considering personal gifts for others back home. Like all major tourist destinations, it is easy to be tempted by the mounds and mounds of things available for purchase that will only inconvenience your return flight. Therefore, while the miniature Eiffel Tower may be enticing, it is best to leave it for those lacking imagination.

Shopping for souvenirs along the Champs-Élysées is a bit disappointing nowadays, as it has been invaded by gift shops in American theme restaurants and varieties of other bland Anglo imperialism. There is something to be said for buying a gift on this famous avenue, but not just any gift is acceptable. Before making a purchase for yourself or others, consider these questions:

1. Is this available at home as well?

2. Does this seem generic?

3. Will I look sophisticated for the purchase?

4. Is there inherent value in purchasing this from the location, or could this be ordered?

5. Is this gift only available in Paris?

6. How truly unique is the purchase?

A few suggestions of specific gifts will help you to determine things for yourself or special people at home, who undoubtedly left you with the parting words of "Bring me something back!" Consider these ideas:

- A tie or other clothing article from a French boutique. Yes, Chanel and Dior are available everywhere, but there is no greater pleasure than walking along Avenue Montaigne, entering a store, and asking to see "*les cravats.*" Of course, this experience may involve paying at least 30 percent more than back home, but there is inherent value in owning something actually from one of these stores. Also, you'll be proud of yourself, and the other tourists will look in awe. Notably, the department store *Printemps* carries not only fashions from around the world but also designers and items that are exclusively French and unavailable elsewhere. If buying something for a special someone back home, in general, anything from one of the above stores will automatically be considered a worthy purchase.

- Think about buying something for your or someone else's home that can be put on display. For your own purchase, think about what you might need at your house/apartment that can be placed conspicuously as a conversation starter. A small vase, a rug, or anything that, when complimented, can evoke the response of "I picked that up the last time I was in Paris." Furthermore, if the purchase is for someone else, think about how great it is to know that when that person is complimented, the response has to include your name.

- While it may seem a bit on the overdone side, a piece of art from a street artist could be a nice addition to any home. The bottom line is, street art is plentiful and inexpensive, but it is easy to lie and inflate the price to friends or claim it was purchased in a gallery. When asked how much it cost, simply say, "Ah, I'd rather not say," and watch the look of respect they give you. This idea is one that the masses generally think about as well; thus, as long as you avoid buying a painting of the Eiffel Tower or a copy of Renoir, you'll look sophisticated.

Souvenirs and gifts may be highly personal investments but consider these options and questions when determining what to buy. If you can't be bothered to shop while in Paris, note also that duty-free at CDG is a great option, provided you have discerning taste. Yes, things may be cheaper this way, and there might be a few nice finds, but is it really necessary to carry five cartons of Marlboros through customs?

Your actions in France will add greatly to the overall experience. Keep in mind the advice in this chapter and the next when planning your *Beyond Your Means* persona and all activities during your trip.

9

The Immersion Method

Now that you've planned all of the side trips and even hit a few "check-offs," it is time to really begin to experience Paris by observing and becoming one with the inhabitants. To outsiders, there can be no more truly fascinating creature than a Frenchman. A stroll down the streets of Paris for the first time is like a trip to the zoo to see exotic animals from a faraway land. At first glance, we share many of the animalistic traits of our distant French cousins, as they too give birth to live young, but there are obvious differences. Like their caged counterparts a barrier exists, albeit invisible, between the French and the Anglo-American world. Curiously, much like how a monkey begins to perform when he notices a group of schoolchildren pointing at him, a Frenchman will happily hop into character when given the opportunity. While a monkey may ravage a banana and throw feces, a flip of the wrist or a dainty sip of coffee can be just as entertaining.

On the banks of the Seine or on the floor of the United Nations, the French will take every opportunity to show others just how good they are at straying from the flock. Often from their perspective, if an idea, concept, or trend is developed outside of France, it necessitates great Gallic improvement or perhaps total condemnation.

The French repeatedly face tough criticism, as illustrated in the tiresome aspersion, "France would be perfect if it wasn't for all the French." But truly, the French merely have their own approach to the world and very strong opinions that shouldn't be quickly dismissed. Any society that can remain proud against a backdrop of so much criticism surely has something to offer.

The essence of being French has caused many opinions to form in every possible circle, from fashion to politics. Thus, preparing for certain peculiarities will help *Beyond Your Means* travelers maximize the experience. The epitome of *Beyond Your Means* traveling is at least feigning an interest in blending with the natives, when necessary, so a brief, casual study will aid in this pursuit.

Les Differences

Paris is a muse for even the most uninspirable, but the aesthetic beauty of the Gallic capital does not come without a price. The French are rarely interested in workaday practicalities interfering with aesthetics; accordingly, Paris can best be viewed as the world's most beautiful painting in a dilapidated frame. To grasp this mindset, contrast the Franco world with the Anglo-American world, where each country's largest cities are designed based on a "sliding scale of convenience."

Keep in mind that what *Europe Beyond Your Means* and most North Americans call "conveniences" might be considered unnecessary clutter and ugliness by our European cousins. Nonetheless, American cities and societal infrastructures are generally planned in such a way to allow maximum convenience for urban dwellers and visitors. Along the Anglo-American linear measure of convenience, the United States and its cities occupy one end, while the United Kingdom and its cities occupy the other. For example, plenty of grocery stores, bars, and restaurants are open on Easter Sunday in Los Angeles, but you might not find many in London.

Cities of other Anglophone countries lie somewhere in between these two points, but neither are necessarily good or bad. Some cultures just prefer things like beauty to convenience, or personal time to economic profit. Individual tastes dictate a preference for running into a neon-lit Dunkin' Donuts embanking a main avenue for your morning coffee versus something more aesthetic that may be tucked away along a side street.

If varying levels of convenience exist between New York and London, then things change completely once the English Channel is crossed. The city of Paris occupies no part of this fictional Anglo-American sliding scale and lies somewhere beyond London like an undiscovered planet in the Kuiper Belt. While some cities might strike a nice compromise between functionality and aesthetics, Paris is not afraid to express an absolute preference for one, resulting in the nearly lifeless condition of the other.

Ultimately, France is like no other place. Being French means being different, or at the very least, it means acting differently in everyday situations. In Anglo-American society, there is a certain order and approach to life's necessities that are recognizable from Chicago to Sydney, distinguished only by a few local interpretations and variances in convenience. But applying this approach to the French world is fruitless. Yes, the French work, and yes, they eat—but differently. The French approach life in a way that cannot plainly be summarized in a few short pages, but understanding the basics will help.

Working

Contrary to popular belief, the French generally do have jobs. They just don't go a lot. But who can blame them? When living in a society that pressures a person to buy fresh bread twice a day, who can find the time? Still, somewhere between their *café au lait* mornings and espresso evenings, many of them do find time to grace an office with their presence.

American society is often described in contrast to French society in that Yanks typically live to work and the French sometimes work, but always live. Even the most minor work reforms in France are often flippantly rejected. Recently, when the French president asked the nation's workers to give up a bank holiday as a "show of solidarity" with the elderly and handicapped, more than half of the nation felt they deserved no solidarity. Because of this stark difference, an understanding of the French working style will provide a helpful foundation for your adventure.

Unlike the dawn-to-dusk productivity typical of Frankfurt and New York, the French workday is structured around the needs of the worker, not the corporation. Below is a fairly template schedule for most of France's hardworking citizens:

- ❑ 10:15 a.m.—Arrive
- ❑ 10: 25 a.m.—Look for boss; exchange pleasantries with boss (if there)
- ❑ 10:30 a.m.—Plan lunch
- ❑ 11:15 a.m.—Cigarette/coffee break
- ❑ 11:35 a.m.—Scoff
- ❑ 11:40 a.m.—Return to desk
- ❑ 11:45 a.m.—Call union representative to complain about working conditions
- ❑ 11:47 a.m.—Turn on computer
- ❑ 12:05 p.m.—Check e-mails from friends
- ❑ 12:10 p.m.—Look good and practice pouty lips
- ❑ 12:25 p.m.—Re-adjust scarf

- ❑ 12:30 p.m.—Second cigarette/coffee break (this time, consider espresso)
- ❑ 12:50 p.m.—Find boss; fictionalize progress of assigned project
- ❑ 1:00 p.m.—Lunch
- ❑ 3:00 p.m.—After-lunch coffee/cigarette break
- ❑ 3:15 p.m.—Ponder just going home
- ❑ 3:20 p.m.—Return to desk
- ❑ 3:25 p.m.—Check voicemail from American counterpart
- ❑ 3:30 p.m.—Giggle with hand effeminately placed over mouth (men and women)
- ❑ 3:40 p.m.—Water-cooler conversation about organizing a walkout
- ❑ 3:50 p.m.—Actual work to support the French economy
- ❑ 4:30 p.m.—Look for co-workers to vent about stress
- ❑ 4:45 p.m.—Plan dinner
- ❑ 5:15 p.m.—Craft e-mails to American counterparts with phrases like "We're working on it" or "Check back later"
- ❑ 5:20 p.m.—Press ignore on calls from U.S. phone numbers
- ❑ 5:55 p.m.—Out the door as fast as the Vichy regime

Too often, the French are criticized for their work habits, which have effectively led to a slowing of their economy since *les Trente Glorieuses*, the thirty-year period of rapid economic expansion following World War II. But perhaps the criticism only stems from a misunderstanding of the culture or even jealousy by those who are forced to deal with problems larger than whether to have one or two *sucrées* on the next coffee break. Therefore, for the rare *Beyond Your Means* traveler who has justified the trip to Paris with work-related purposes, understanding this daily schedule, coupled with some other advice, will make the transition smooth.

Tips on Working in France

- Attendance should be sporadic.

- Stagger vacation time with others so that productivity will be minimal for months.

- The French love hierarchy, so be sure to follow a chain of command, when appropriate.

- Discuss the possibility of a strike on at least a weekly basis.

- Count your "sick days" as holidays that should be taken before the end of the calendar year.

Neither the French nor *Beyond Your Means* practitioners have much interest in working, so moving towards more leisure-focused pursuits is a necessary next step. Cognizance of the following cultural caveats will undoubtedly enhance your Parisian adventure.

Eating

French cuisine is the most legendary in all the world, and a great deal of time is spent at meals or planning them. Volumes have been written on both French dining etiquette and the absolute top cuisine in hidden locations throughout the country. Because non-natives must accept the fact that eating is a fine art to the French that takes a lifetime to master, a crash course is necessary to understand the cuisine culture.

On the issue of etiquette, never forget to bring an offering when dining at a friend's home. Also, as with anywhere, it is naturally recommended to avoid gifts that conjure up negative memories; thus, consider that in France, chrysanthemums are a flower reserved exclusively for cemeteries, so bringing them to dinner would be like bringing Jell-O shooters to an AA meeting.

Be sure to sample everything, and eat all that is on your plate since, to the French, leaving something on your plate is like visiting the Louvre for the first time and not seeing the Mona Lisa. Do not misinterpret this as gluttony, however, as the French are known for eating rather lightly. Note that portions are drastically smaller than most other Western nations; thus, consuming all of the incredibly fatty foods offered to you is perfectly suitable. Don't worry about the fat content in anything, as the smaller portions, excessive wine, and leisurely pace at which people eat have led to a lower level of heart disease known as the French paradox. Remember that appropriately named literature like *Why French Women Don't Get Fat* is based in truth. As a cardinal rule, even gluttonous *Beyond Your Means* travelers will lose weight in France, due to these epicurean peculiarities.

There are several French delicacies that may not sit well with a foreign palate. You might have to go to Mongolia at this point to find someone who has not heard that *escargot* are garlic-sautéed snails, but culinary adventures are always worth the risk in France. Paris has access to the best food products as well as the best chefs on the planet. If it's on the menu in Paris, it's probably worth trying. Assume that if no one actually enjoyed it and no one bothered to order it, it would have been removed from the menu long ago. For the most authentic experience, consider sampling these items, but remember these translations for some of the more "exotic" dishes:

- Boudin: Common also in Louisiana, this translates to blood sausage.

- Cervelle: One word—brains. Typically, lamb or veal, but brains nonetheless.

- Civelles: Baby eels that are eaten raw.

Dining Out

There are many points at which the best advice is to preserve your euros for other *Beyond Your Means* pursuits, but food is not one of them. At every opportunity available, you should visit new restaurants and practice indulgence until your heart's content. Because of the intricate role that food plays in the society, to embrace France is to eat…a lot.

The list of great restaurants in Paris is impossible to exhaust and is also ever changing. The "it" restaurants are as unpredictable as next season's *haute couture*. But consider of few of these time-honored standbys:

- **Le Bristol:** Home to the world's best lobster, this classy establishment is part of a five-star hotel. Try not to be too obnoxious when consuming the bread, but keep in mind that it is exported to as far away as the Royal Palace in Bangkok. Dress is business, and reservations are a near must.
  Address: 112, rue du Faubourg St Honoré, Paris 75008
  Phone: +33.53.43.43.00
  Métro: Champs-Élysées-Clemenceau

- **Brasserie Bofinger:** This restaurant has been known for its ocean-fresh shellfish and Alsatian-style sauerkraut for nearly 150 years. An outdoor dining option exists for those who would prefer this experience. The dress is business casual, and reservations are recommended.

  Address: 7, rue de la Bastille, Paris 75004
  Phone: +33.42.72.87.82
  Métro: Bastille

- **Guy Savoy:** One of the most honored and famous restaurants in Paris. Highlights include a wine selection of over eight hundred choices and the menu *dégustation*. Grilled pigeon, oysters, and a variety of other specialties are sure to please. Predictably, reservations are required.

Address: 18, rue Troyon, Paris, 75017
Phone: +33.43.80.40.61
Métro: Charles de Gaulle-Etoile or Ternes

- **Maxim's:** Arguably one of the most famous high-end restaurants in the world. Maxim's has been serving up famous crêpes, lamb, and French decadence since the 1800s. Nowadays, there are several Maxim's around the globe, but Paris is home to the original that has been etched in popular culture and is an established gathering spot for the *Beyond Your Means* crowd, as well as for the within-your-means folk.

    Address: 3, Rue Royale, Paris, 75008
    Phone: 01 42 65 27 94
    Métro: Concorde

- **Le Dôme**: Known far and wide for its seafood, the bouillabaisse is considered to be the best in Paris. The crowd at *Le Dôme* is very sophisticated, consisting of politicians and artists alike. Patrons are expected to be rather dressy, and reservations are recommended.

    Address: 108, bd du Montparnasse, Paris, 75014
    Phone: +33.43.35.25.81
    Métro: Vavin or Edgar Quinet

While the *Beyond Your Means* lifestyle embraces spending too much money on meals, eventually credit cards will reach their limits and parents will stop believing that your wallet was stolen. Therefore, consider a few techniques to experience the best food that Paris has to offer without facing embarrassment and giving a French waiter the satisfaction of telling you that your credit card is *diminué.*

In many cases, some restaurants have taken a page from the cabarets and offer a cheaper option for customers who sit at the bar. This dining experience may not be ideal but will give you a chance to see and be seen. A further option may be to go to the restaurant for only a *refreshment,* appetizer, or dessert. Remember that paying too much for these insubstantial options is much less harmful to your credit rating than paying too much for an entire meal, the only drawback being the inevitable pernicious stare from the waiter when asking for *l'addition* after such a light noshing.

Still, many restaurants will offer cheaper locations that are attached to the main establishment or are at least close enough for you to be seen mingling with the crowd who doesn't even consider the price. For example, *Le Dôme* offers *Le Bistrot du Dôme*, which provides a great meal without the heartbreaking bill of its namesake. If choosing to dine at *Le Bistrot du Dôme*, it is in no way a lie to tell your friends about your evening at "*Le Dôme.*"

Besides the famous restaurants that should be sampled, take into account a few fair warnings. To have the true French culinary experience, keep in mind the many eating habits that are, by definition, anti-French.

Anti-French Eating

- **Buffets:** The word is French; the concept is not. Aside from a few rest-stop restaurants along the highway, designed specifically to attract American tourists, there is no equivalent to the all-you-can-eat family dining establishment.

- **Places to Avoid:** A fundamental principle is to avoid any restaurant with a laminated menu or with someone hustling you from outside. Remember, there are reasons for both of these issues. Laminated menus mean the restaurant never changes its selections, and outside hustlers are necessary because the food isn't good enough to bring people in without pressure. Also, be especially leery of any restaurant with a "book" menu when looking for more upscale dining. These places typically dedicate three to four pages for their entire menu and then duplicate it in sixteen different languages. Obviously, then, they are not able to add to the menu very often, as this would require hiring a team of translators, reprinting/re-laminating every page, and rebinding their irreverent culinary bibles. Eating is a strict religion in France and heretical restaurants are marked with scarlet letters like laminated menus or outside hustlers.

- **Greasy Spoons:** Don't expect to find "Moons Over My Hammy" or the Rooty-Tooty-Fresh-'N-Fruity lifestyle anywhere in France.

- **Doggy Bags:** What you don't eat at the restaurant stays at the restaurant.

- **Soft Drinks:** Don't order these with a nice meal. France is the country that produces the world's finest wines, so take advantage. Besides, free refills of "cola light" do not exist, and there is rarely any ice. If you're a teetotaler or need to detox after multiple *guelle de bois* (hangovers), just stick with water. Steak just doesn't wash down quite as smoothly with Fanta.

- **Entrée is the Appetizer:** As is sometimes the case, a difference in a word or two can be distracting and ruin the meal, so keep in mind that the French term for appetizer is *entrée*, and the French word for entree is *plat principal* or simply *plat*.

- Restaurants without French Menus: While it is safe to say that all French restaurants will have menus in the lingua franca of the nation, restaurants such as Planet Hollywood on the Champs-Élysées have been known to use an English menu as the default. In this case, Beyond Your Means travelers must ask the question, "What's the point?"

Superfluous Kissing

The French love *faire la bise* as a greeting, a good-bye or for anything else. This catches many non-Europeans, who prefer their personal space, off guard. There is much debate among the non-French over when it is appropriate to kiss and when it isn't. As a general rule, allow the French person to take control for determining when a kiss or a handshake is appropriate, especially in mixed-gender greetings.

Always remember that the type of kiss used for a greeting in no way resembles the misnamed "French kiss." Intense research has revealed that inserting one's tongue in the mouth of a stranger is offensive in many cultures, including France. And, for the record, a slap feels the same everywhere.

Lack of Space

When asked about this personal space issue, any Parisian might retort with a knee-jerk reaction that "Dis iz only *le problème* for *le* fat American!" *Au contraire, mon frère.* The French value personal space slightly less than, say, the English or the Germans, and much less than the dreaded Americans. There is no place in France where this is more evident than in Paris.

Nearly everyone has been to their local history museum as a child, seen the armor used by medieval knights, and inevitably remarked how small people once were. For some reason, Parisians have continued to employ this sizing model in their planning. The size of chairs or seats in the most common places are more appropriate for men and women who lived at least three hundred to four hundred years ago. Furthermore, a typical café has the seats belonging to adjacent tables sitting right next to one another. This makes it nearly impossible not to receive or deliver a stray elbow at some point during a meal or *apéritif*. Prepare for toilets, hotels, restaurants, and many other places to make you feel as if you have taken a voyage to Lilliput or the Lollipop Guild, rather than a trip to Paris. Some grown men become expert contortionists when trying to negotiate the use of a Parisian toilet, which many hardened criminals swear is merely a Chinese solitary confinement cell with a loo placed inside.

However, many *Beyond Your Means* travelers frequent hotels and restaurants far outside of their price ranges and rarely encounter such problems. Thus, the lack of appreciable personal space may merely be a cute anomaly encountered only *de temps en temps*, rather than a constant annoyance. It has been said that one can swim in the bathrooms at *Le George V*, but it's difficult to find space to store toothpaste near the tap at that one-star Rick recommended. Remain advised that many "hostiles" have gang showers, rather than even cramped facilities. These are obviously much more spacious in one sense—oh, what fun.

French Gyms

Anyone who has casually flipped through the channels and seen ESPN's World's Strongest Man competition has probably noticed that there are rarely, if ever, any competitors from France. Parisian gyms are a good indication of why. Working out in Paris is more about telling other people you visited the physical structure than accomplishing any meaningful activity. Unlike a metropolitan American or English gym, the "cardio" sections are not packed with females clamoring over the elliptical machines to burn off those excess calories consumed the previous day. Weight-room equipment can be hopelessly outdated and appear more like what existed in someone's suburban basement in the 1970s than the top-of-the-line machines you might be used to. Either way, it hardly matters. When Parisians do exercise, they are much more inclined to run outside, rather than confine themselves indoors. However, moving at any pace above a stroll is considered taboo to many, which French president Nicholas Sarkozy learned shortly after being elected, when he faced daily criticism for his jogging routine. The French public labeled his jogging as "crass" and even "right wing." Famed philosopher Alain Finkielkraut went as far as to call jogging "undignified."

Despite these opinions on jogging, Parisians are quite fond of swimming, but facilities are rare and often very crowded. Paris was built at a time when taking a bath was considered hazardous to your health, so it's no real surprise that city planners didn't predict that people might one day want to jump into huge tanks of water *en masse*. Dedicated *Beyond Your Means* exercise enthusiasts should plan to hit the gym or the pool at some point after lunch or the mid-morning, when patronage is at its lowest.

Drinking

The French, as a Latin culture, do not drink for the sole purpose of getting drunk; getting drunk just happens—*c'est la vie*. As long as drunkenness wasn't the original purpose, the behavior is more readily excused. Incidentally, the term "bender" has infiltrated the nomenclature of the youth. Meaning, Paris still has its share of imbibers who can be found at actual bars, rather than cafés or restaurants.

An oddity that most don't realize right away is that unlike the rest of the world, beer in France is often more expensive than wine at a café or bar. Many tourists don't ever learn this, so *Beyond Your Means* travelers have the added benefit of appearing much more indulgent than they really are by posing with a glass of Pinot Noir, rather than with a bottle of 1664.

In general, national pride and taste usually dictate that Parisians stay within borders for their libations, but this is not a steadfast rule. Unlike an Anglo bar, where you'll find people sucking down vast quantities of different cocktails, when Parisians consider non-domestic concoctions, they tend to stick with what they know best from the international market place—whiskey. *Beyond Your Means* analysts have tried to find a concrete cultural reason as to why, but have yet to discover one. An admiration for Tennessee has been ruled out, however. All that our researchers do know is that certain alcoholic staples from other lands remain unrecognized. Vodka on the rocks? Unheard of. Rum and Coke? No way. Gin and tonic? Too English. But whiskey … whiskey in all its variations is a nearly exclusive companion of the Parisian heavy-drinking culture. It's far from uncommon to enter a bar in Paris and see a table of twentysomethings gulping down Jack Daniel's on the rocks. Who says they truly hate America?

If the mood arises late at night for additional alcohol reserves, remember that Paris does not have twenty-four-hour drive-thru daiquiri stores like its unruly stepchild, New Orleans. A wine shop won't be open past 8:00 p.m., and *supermarchés* are long closed. There are two options late at night: any of the surprisingly plentiful Arab food shops that now dot the streets, or an open café. Unfamiliar to most, cafés are more than willing to sell bottles of wine off their menus and let you leave without a classy brown paper bag. This is quite a handy tip that gives even more credence to the phrase "over-served."

Also, always remember that wine shops are not open on Sundays—at all. Again, the Arab food shops come in handy on the Christian holy day. Do not expect a wine shop in your area to re-open after church services have concluded, because it most certainly will not. Remember, when in Paris, applying a strict profit-and-loss mentality will continually place you in the bottom percentile of the class. Thus, if you're waiting until Sunday to purchase that bottle of Cognac you promised your father—well, to borrow the colloquial, you're shit out of luck.

Smoking

One of the many manifestations of how the French approach the developed world on their own terms is their position on smoking. Instead of falling lockstep with many other nations, French smoking rates among youth have actually been increasing in recent years. Basically, the French love to smoke and do so with Old World elegance that is a far cry from many modern images of downtrodden lung hackers. As with most things, the French exercise self-control, so the associated health problems are not as prevalent.

Still, the French have not escaped smoking bans. A nationwide smoking ban for public places was passed in 2006. Smoking is still permitted in bars, cafés, and nightclubs in hermetically sealed rooms. Many companies, however, have taken this opportunity to develop VIP-style smoking rooms with an "air" of exclusivity. The French love exclusivity, so this loophole may defeat a main purpose of the ban, since many could be enticed to light up.

While smoking is terrible for your health and could result in death, it is yet another way to take part in French culture. While Philip Morris brands (like Marlboro) have made great strides in the European market, there is still nothing more French than puffing on a *Gauloises*. Even the *Gauloises* pack is a throwback to the Revolution, as it proudly proclaims "*Liberté Toujours*" (Freedom Always). This particular brand, despite now being manufactured in Spain, was named for early French heroes and was long produced in France. *Gauloises* was the favorite of Jean-Paul Sartre and countless characters from film and literature who were thought to embody France.

Furthermore, the French smoking style is markedly different from the rapid, nervous puffing seen in other countries. A simple light drag followed by either placing the cigarette out of the way in an ashtray or gently holding it to the side, while continuing on with conversation, are the preferred ways to light up. Incidentally, most cigarettes available in France are a much heavier smoke than what is available in North America.

Idiosyncrasies are part of the French zeitgeist in the way that rock 'n' roll is central to Americana. Preparing for the curiosities of the culture and the differences in which the French take pride helps a traveler to go a long way toward accepting the country and the people. But while accepting cultural differences is one thing, preparing for the inconveniences that result from them is another matter altogether.

Preparing for Inconveniences

The many differences between Anglo and Franco cultures lend themselves to a host of inconveniences for visitors. Fortunately, when visiting other occidental nations like France, the inconveniences are more quirky, as opposed to life-threatening. Because of the inherent differences in what Parisians hold in high esteem, there are certain things that may seem intolerably inconvenient and even absurd. But hey, that's Paris.

The Paris Métro

The Paris Métro is often heralded as the most thorough underground mass-transit system in the world. This, by no means, makes it anywhere close to dependable. To many observers, it is not precisely clear what the French government pays the Parisian Métro workers to do. Is it to stay home and strike, or run the trains? There is no obvious answer as to what they actually spend more time doing.

In the spirit of fairness, it is interesting to look at Paris in terms of its peer cities, in relation to passenger convenience. New York MTA workers will think long and hard about having a transit strike, knowing that the public could easily turn against them. The uniformed men and women of the London Tube publish potential strike dates well ahead of time; acknowledging the problems their personal grievances might have on a large number of people. Conversely, Parisian Métro *ouvriers* will justify a strike just because it's a Tuesday and four guys suggested it on a coffee break yesterday afternoon. So steadfast is the commitment to strike that in 2005, when the Olympic committee came to judge Paris as a potential host city for the 2012 Games, Métro workers decided that there was no better way to show off the city's dependable infrastructure than to call a one-day strike; the Games were awarded to London—imagine that.

Remember the idea that in some ways, Paris can be like camping? Just be prepared to hike, no matter when you visit; the walk around is more inspiring than the Métro anyway.

As an aside, the majority of *Beyond Your Means* researchers actually idolize the audacity of the Paris Métro employees, because of the value placed on getting paid to not go to work. Unfortunately, though, our think-tank researchers have American "at will" employment status.

To be completely honest, when functioning, the Paris Métro is incredibly well run. Comparatively, it costs very little, has short waiting times, and allows travel to basically anywhere in the city quite quickly.

Lack of Service

Another of the noted inconveniences Paris has to offer is a profound lack of service. Referring back to linear measure of convenience, Paris might frustrate those accustomed to attentive wait staff or hotel reception in North America. As most everyone knows by now, European waiters are not paid in tips, which means *Roland* can't be expected to appear every couple of minutes to make sure everything is all right in the same way that Courtney does at the T.G.I. Friday's back home. However, by moving up the restaurant star-ratings scale, the differences in service begin to diminish, until reaching the top, where nothing is appreciably different—the bottom and middle are where the rampant frustration lies.

Store Hours: *Liberté, égalité …?*

The limited store hours are rarely something North American transplants can accept or understand. For some unknown reason, most businesses, other than restaurants and bars, shut promptly in the early evening, around six or seven o'clock. Sure, sport fashion shops in Les Halles stay open a lot later, but readers of this book probably don't care where they can buy the latest Puma fashions before a "plastic maxing" evening. The general rule is that the nicer the boutique, the more promptly they close, regardless of what you offer to spend or who you might be (just ask Oprah).

This weird economic construct poses an interesting question about French society and commerce: are they subconsciously trying to keep the middle class away from the luxurious effects of life, or is it that they really don't see why anyone might want to swing by Louis Vuitton after work? The first assumption seems rather socially repressive, while the second appears to blatantly ignore economics. Normal tourists rarely encounter any problem, though, but *Beyond Your Means* travelers should take notice. If you wake up after noon and eventually slither onto the end of a four-hour line at the *Tour Eiffel* on your last day, there probably won't be time to do that shopping on the Champs-Élysées that you promised yourself and others.

Some trappings of more service-oriented conveniences have infiltrated Paris, for better or for worse. Take the chain *boulangerie* "Paul," for example. Paul has a similar history and technique to Starbucks. It started out as an unorthodox small bakery in Lille and now has a store on every corner in Paris. Paul has set prices, a fairly large selection, and quickly moving lines. Similarly, what Paul lacks in imagination and actual authenticity, it makes up for in raw efficiency and a standardized product. Paul could, however, become inconvenient as well. It will be difficult to find any small, inconspicuous, out-of-the-way bakeries nestled on one of the side streets in the Marais, as Paul has put so many other *boulangeries* out of business. Paul also still closes at a ridiculously early hour, making it inconvenient in its own right, especially since it is now the only option in many parts of town.

Heatstroke Acceptance

Even if the great protectors of *l'esprit français* have momentarily turned their heads and unwittingly allowed some modern conveniences to infiltrate the cultural citadel that is Paris, finding a modern way to deal with the stifling heat is not one of them. *Europe Beyond Your Means* has searched for an answer to this peculiar stance on heatstroke acceptance and has concluded that Parisians must simply like trying to emulate their revolutionary heroes by relishing the intense heat and sweaty stinkiness that plagued the peasant classes for centuries and helped fuel a revolution. Understandably, installing *climatisé* would take too much time away from basking in self-glory. It is also possible the French may be refusing to notice that every consecutive summer dethrones the previous year's temperatures and becomes "the hottest summer on record." Either way, Paris is a nearly unbearable place when the mercury rises above 85°F (30°C). The streets are small and cramped, and housing is mysteriously set up to allow the minimum possible airflow, thus only intensifying the effect. No wonder so many died in the plague.

This being the case, July and August are by far the hottest months—yet the most popular to visit Paris. During this time, the city is littered with tourists, while the real Parisians are often taking refuge elsewhere in the country.

When assessing "How bad is it really going to be?" remember that Parisian cafés are open-air affairs. There is usually no cool and air-conditioned indoor option. Normally, all the windows and doors are flung open during the summer, sometimes making it hotter inside than out. The choice then presents itself: sit outside in the scorching sun or inside to enjoy the hot stuffiness of the stale air, as Paris rarely has a breeze in the summer.

Fear not—while the Parisians are not willing to go American with their heat problems, they are willing to compromise. Many cafés now have cool mists of water that spray over patrons every few minutes that provide temporary relief from the unendurable conditions.

Trying to Appear French

After becoming comfortable with certain cultural differences, travelers are ready to attempt "appearing French." Entire classes could be developed to train someone in the fine art of appearing French, but since *Beyond Your Means* travelers aren't known for advance preparation, a couple ideas on how to approach cultural immersion will be helpful. Being French can never be mastered by a foreigner, but try these approaches in your attempt to gain acceptance.

Protest Something ... Anything

The French may have a reputation for being docile, but quite often, the citizens cast aside their refinement and take to the streets. While not all protests have led to beheadings, the protests of May 1968 nearly led to the overthrow of the De Gaulle government, and protests in recent years over the idea of (gasp!) at-will employment brought the country to a temporary standstill. Ultimately, it doesn't take much to ignite an uprising. To properly assimilate, try starting your own revolution or at least paint a protest sign or two. If you aren't confident in your French writing abilities, then leave the sign blank and just copy someone else's at the rally. There is usually a large-scale protest about something or other once a week in Paris, so you should have no reason to put this obligation off for too long.

Strike a Pose

Perhaps the biggest part of being French is believing that the world is always watching you. Each Frenchman, at least in part, views himself as being like the Eiffel Tower—standing proudly, completely erect, as an object of great admiration. Like the great art on display in France's many museums, the French people themselves feel as if they are living sculptures commanding immense awe and approbation. To be French is to feel worthy of notice. Therefore, whether standing or walking, allowing others to bask in your greatness is sure to earn you immersion points.

Avoid *Supermarchés*

Nowadays, almost anything can be purchased in a major supermarket in Paris. For many years the French resisted the supermarket concept, even going so far as to ban these establishments from advertising on television. The ban has been lifted, but the latent disapproval of supermarkets is omnipresent. To appear French, resist the temptation to go to the same store for peanut butter, bread, Q-tips, and toe-nail clippers, and instead, visit the small shops that specialize in certain products. If you must go to the *supermarchés* because you are rushed, feel free to lie to your family and others about where you picked up any of the goods you purchase. *Supermarchés* in Paris can be compared to adult video stores: they are always busy, but no one admits to shopping there.

Have an Opinion on Everything

Every Frenchman has an opinion on everything. Even if the topic is new to the world stage, a Frenchman will defend his particular position with the vehemence of deeply held religious devotion. To be French is to be opinionated and to find a way to invoke that opinion through any possible measure. For confirmation on this, just ask representatives of any other permanent member nation of the United Nations Security Council.

In recent years, the French government has gone so far as funding *France Vingt-Quatre* (France 24), a round-the-clock international news station to rival the BBC and CNN International to ensure the French perspective on world events is considered. In due course, to appear French, it is imperative to develop strong and slightly skewed beliefs on every possible subject, ranging in importance from international armed conflicts to cheese tariffs, and be prepared to engage in existential *tête-à-tête* to defend those views.

This passion carries over from dinnertime conversation to the real world. In all seriousness, French politicians and diplomats are well known for their preparation and abilities. French presidents rarely use notes when speaking, and diplomats are trained in special schools to fine tune their skills. Worldwide, diplomats and politicians aspire to be a "Talleyrand" for a reason.

Complain … a Lot

In general, things are pretty good in France, but much like the high school girl who personifies the nation, unnecessary complaining is anything but unnecessary. The coffee is always too hot or too cold, the baguette is too stale, or the wine hasn't been given an opportunity to breathe. The French approach to most things is that there is always room for improvement. This philosophy has good points, but can be frustrating.

Perhaps the part of life with which the French take the most issue is the stress of the workday. If trying to gain favor with the natives is a priority, then train yourself to believe that national productivity really would be higher if workers were able to fully recuperate throughout the year. For example, practice casually bringing up that five weeks of paid vacation just isn't enough anymore, given the effect of the stressful globalized world.

Give the French the Respect to which They Feel Entitled

In order to be accepted by *les francaise* while in their country, the French must be given proper deference. While you may not think it necessary to praise them or talk about their superior art and cuisine, they think they are entitled. Be sure to compliment at least one aspect of the French culture in every conversation. *Beyond Your Means* etiquette indicates that for every time you misspeak their native language, offer one compliment of their culture.

Develop a Parisian Disposition

Beyond fashion, Parisians have a certain look that imposters must master before they can fool anyone. Elements of this look include limiting smiling and never looking favorably at a stranger on the street. Also, learning to make a cup of coffee last for several hours is particularly useful. Moreover, avoid walking, and instead, try to develop your own sashay, saunter, or glide. But first and foremost, learn to give a subtle scoff at all things, even those that should generally be pleasant. Kittens, children, and senior citizens are as equally deserving of a scoff as jeans-shorted tourists.

After mastering a few rudiments, the final test in appearing Parisian is having the strength. when approached for directions on the street. to utter in a heavy accent, "I don't speak English."

Learning to appear French is quite a difficult task, since those who have perfected the persona have been trained from birth. The French are instilled with a sense of entitlement that sets them apart from the rest of the world. Familiarizing yourself with their quirks and eccentricities before landing at Charles de Gaulle will ensure a better trip and set you on your way to properly imitating the populace.

For whatever differences may exist, the best advice possible is to truly immerse yourself and go with it. The best part of *vacances* is not doing things that you typically do at home and being able to escape the inhibitions and restrictions of the daily grind. While in Paris, live by the notion that "Convenience is for those with obligations to others than themselves," and accept the French for the intriguing people that they are.

10

French *Fries?*
A Guide to an American Day in Paris

Traveling for any extended period usually means that times will arise where one requires refreshment in their own culture. Paris provides a perpetually captivating set of circumstances, but there may be moments when a yearning for that home field cannot be shaken. After days or weeks of doing things the French way, *Beyond Your Means* travelers may require a small sojourn away from the little cafés, elegant wines, and sensible portions. Basically, sometimes France is just a little too French.

Within the Western world, perhaps the most non-French culture of all is that offered by the land of fast food, public drunkenness, and fad diets: the United States of America. Even non-Americans may want to partake in a bit of American culture in Paris, just to try something new.

Early signs of this desire to act like an American typically begin a couple of days or weeks before the victim actually succumbs to the urge. You find yourself walking along streets, no longer mesmerized by Paris, eyeing things like French versions of hot dogs, wondering if they will be able to extinguish the craving. Or it may be evident when deciding that you can't masquerade as "Euro" anymore, and you return to your place of lodging to spend an afternoon kitted out in a polo shirt, khaki shorts, and flip-flops.

Since all visitors to Paris may enjoy a brief flirtation with Yankee Doodle, this chapter has been dedicated to places, pastimes, and peculiarities that are rooted in America or will undoubtedly involve Americans. After holding hands with Uncle Sam, it will be much easier to fall back in love with France.

Instead of spending hours in agony, trying to hide your problem or trying to ignore it, *Europe Beyond Your Means* has prepared an itinerary for the perfect American Day in Paris. This plan will help you either end all of your cravings for apple pie and the Statue of Liberty or, at the very least, do some things that are, by design, non-French.

Europe Beyond Your Means suggests a one-day American cultural immersion to smother this lust for something that isn't French. It is necessary to attack the urge directly, rather than hoping it will subside or treating it gradually. Piecemeal attempts to taste America could result in disappointing weekly meals at Café Indiana or continuing to buy Parisian "New York Style Pizza" (yuk) in the streets. Dragging out a slow cure over the course of several days or weeks to kill this longing for home, or something different, would be just plain foolish. Having a daily dose of American-brand living may help you, but doing so will only destroy your "street cred" as a *Beyond Your Means* traveler in Paris. Friends and locals will see you constantly holding souvenir cups from international chain restaurants or scarfing down fast food in the street. The best advice is to be as American as possible all in one day, thus putting the plague in remission for at least a few weeks and fortifying the fictitious international character you've work so hard to create. Before embarking, there are a few additional tips to keep in mind:

- If a little homesickness or desire to be non-French arises early in a trip, do not waste an American Day too early. At least ten days of Parisian life are necessary before issuing your "declaration of the rights" to meatloaf.

- Keep a running list of places you've seen that look like they will be packed with full-bellied capitalists. Heaven forbid that you forget about wanting an extra-thick chocolate shake when you most need it.

- America is all about bulk, so try to assemble as many friends as possible to join in the festivities.

- Public relations is key when trying to convince others to join in the fun. Remember, many may still be battling their own internal demons since, realistically, everyone comes to terms with the reality of their passport origin at different times. Therefore, everyone might not be comfortable at the same time as you are with uttering the sentence, "I want a number one—and supersize it!"

If you have taken these points to heart and know that today is to be the American Day, hold nothing back and begin your Star-Spangled Adventure shortly after daybreak.

Where to Be American

Doing anything that is strictly American that doesn't involve food is difficult, because food is so much a part of American culture. If you've been in Paris for a month or longer, there is no doubt that the hunger pangs are proving to be almost intolerable. But activities other than eating are essential to getting all the American urges out of your system.

One commonality with the French and American cultures is that both involve cheese. The French type of cheese, however, involves the milk of various mammals, while the American type generally involves wearing Mickey Mouse ears. In order to be American and sample the cheese you have been longing for, visiting sites that are overflowing with Americans should be helpful.

You can probably do nothing to celebrate the spirit of America more than by visiting Jim Morrison's grave at *Père-Lachaise* cemetery. Countless numbers of Americans (as well as other foreigners) visit the Lizard King's grave to get drunk/stoned and subsequently urinate, sleep, or burn wax all over it. It is also, evidentially, quite normal to leave Jim half-empty bottles of whiskey or other spirits. Nothing says baseball and hot apple pie like stoned, half-naked, middle-class white kids having a party in a graveyard.

Aside from the antics surrounding the main attraction, *Père-Lachaise* is one of the most famous cemeteries in the world and would be worth a visit otherwise. It is located in the 20th arrondissement, which makes it an ideal stop after breakfast. It is widely reputed to be the world's most visited cemetery because of the other notables buried there. It is the final resting place for Oscar Wilde and Édith Piaf, as well as many other icons of French culture. But honestly, on American Day these graves shouldn't be visited when more time can be spent with Jim.

Notably, this is the perfect spot to supplement another nation's tourist attractions. For instance, any British members of your party who were willing to acquiesce to American Day might want to skip the whole psychedelic tour and visit the *Pont de l'Alma*, where Princess Diana was tragically killed. There is a bit of irony in this, though. While the Brits will be abstaining from certain

American relics, they will be forced to pay respect to their princess at a replica of the Statue of Liberty's torch. This was given to Paris by the United States as a gift during the centennial celebration of the original statue. Pedestrians, as easily imagined, are not allowed to go into the actual tunnel where Diana died, so this has become the next best thing. Assuredly, paying homage to Princess Diana and visiting Liberty's torch will provide opportunities for everyone to discuss amber waves of grain. After all, the French haven't always hated Old Glory.

American culture and American leaders go in and out of style in Paris, just like fashion. What the French totally commit to loving for all of eternity can be detested in mere moments. Fortunately for Americans, the period surrounding the American Revolution was one such period in which American leaders and concepts could do no wrong. Because of this, there are two statues in the 16th arrondissement dedicated to Benjamin Franklin and George Washington. Neither of these will provide the same debacle you doubtlessly suffered through at the Morrison gravesite. The statue of General Washington can be found in the center of *Place d'Iéna* (*Métro Iéna*) near Avenue de New York. Benjamin Franklin can be found by proceeding just a little farther to a small park at *Trocadero*. Franklin was an extremely popular diplomat in Paris in the years following the American Revolution. Washington was worthy of a statue for no other reason than he defeated the British, the historical equivalent to a back-to-back winning of the World Cup. This is why he is depicted as General Washington rather than as president. There are also countless plaques throughout the city marking the homes where Jefferson, Adams, and others resided as diplomats during the early years of the American republic.

The French also have a habit of naming streets after other American leaders, such as Avenue du President Wilson and Avenue du Franklin Roosevelt, since they found reasons to like the United States after the world wars. These iconoclasts aside, proceeding to the next American object in Paris should have even the most unpatriotic travelers placing hand over heart.

The French gave the Statue of Liberty to the Americans as a gift to commemorate one hundred years of independence. The Americans, thinking of no better gift to give the French for the hundredth birthday of their republic, gave back a replica of the same gift…only a lot smaller. The thoughtfulness and creativity of the gift obviously speaks for itself. The knock-off Statue of Liberty now stands near *Grenelle Bridge* on the *Île des Cygnes* on an island between the 16th and 7th arrondissements. Dedicated on November 15,

1889, it looks toward its "larger sister" in New York Harbor, which had been erected three years earlier.

Saluting the Culinary Flag of the Stars and Stripes

Much like the French, a signature component to American life is food. Well, it isn't so much the food that is part of the American culture as the vast consumption of it. From coffee and donuts to catfish and fries, Americans love to eat. For the perfect American Day, you must be prepared to eat as much as possible.

Life Between the Buns

There is no way American Day can truly be complete without a visit to the most shining example of Americana—McDonald's. Before giving a list of other locations to indulge in American fare, remember that at least one visit to McDonald's is essential for any American Day. You can start or end your day there, or visit it on four separate occasions, but giving proper deference to Mayor McCheese and the Hamburglar is required.

Listing all the Micky D's locations in Paris is pointless, since walking around in any direction will eventually lead to one. Also, on any given day, a McDonald's may be identified by the large number of French farmers spraying manure on the golden arches to protest globalization. Anytime you see tractors and farm vehicles assembling in Paris, just follow them, as this will likely lead to a McDonald's. But hurry, as once they arrive, the hash browns will no longer taste the same.

Parisians may claim to hate American fast food, but for some reason, more and more of these chain restaurants continue to establish themselves. *Europe Beyond Your Means* suggests indulging in as much variety as possible. Remember: the point of American Day is to get the cravings out of your system in one fell swoop.

That being said, there are a plethora of American fast-food restaurants from which to choose. The biggest of these, after Fat-Donald's, are the nutritional staples of KFC, Subway, and Pizza Hut. These establishments are spread throughout the city like little embassies in the hostile territory of Gallic cuisine. Unfortunately, Parisians have yet to embrace the concept of a "food court," so you might not be able to hit all three in one spot, but there are several locations where one is not that far away from the others. Do not be fooled by European fast-food restaurants, like Quick Burger, masquerading as the genuine article. Quick Burger is far inferior to any American fast-food restaurant in terms of quality, taste, and especially speed of service (the name alone is pure fiction).

Sadly, Burger King closed its doors in France back in 1997, and Wendy's does not maintain a presence outside of North America, so the aforementioned four are your best choices.

Breakfast

The first order of business is to get a cup of coffee; therefore, you will proceed directly to one of the greatest examples of American capitalism and destroyer of local variety known to man—Starbucks. Not all Starbucks are created equally; based on their location, some have a greater concentration of American clientele than others. The French claim to hate Starbucks and wish it had never been introduced to their country, but strangely, the stores are profitable and new ones are continually opening. There are actually over twenty stores in Paris, which is no small accomplishment, considering *café* is fundamentally the French national sport. *Europe Beyond Your Means* recommends two Starbucks in particular that have a reputation of being nearly exclusively American.

Particularly American Starbucks

34 Quai du Louvre	91 Boulevard Saint Germain
Paris, PRS 75001	Paris, PRS 75006
Métro: Musée du Louvre	Métro: Odeon

Either of these will be a great place to begin and plan out the itinerary for your day, while greeting numerous other American tourists in line and thumbing through a *USA Today*. The whole visit to Starbucks is slightly ironic, considering it was started by people who liked the concept of Italian and French coffee bars so much that they brought it to America. Don't get hung up on the details, though; after all, democracy came from Greece, and hot dogs were imported from Germany.

Just like in the United States, after coffee you will require breakfast. The tall *latté* should act only as a pick-me-up and an advertisement to locals on the street to beware, as no matter what the date might be, it is your personal Independence Day.

If you're not going to go the whole way and can't bring yourself to consume the top of the hydrogenated fats pyramid but still want to do it right, then consider "Breakfast in America." This authentic American diner was started by a native of Connecticut, filling a void in the market he saw after moving to Paris. It started with one location in the Latin Quarter but has since expanded to the other side of the river as well. In the American tradition, Breakfast in America serves a breakfast all day long that can easily outrank the Egg McMuffin, in taste if not in symbolism. Check out these locations and visit the Web site for more information: www.breakfast-in-america.com.

Breakfast in America (locations)

Rive Gauche	Rive Droite
17, rue des Ecoles, Paris, 75005	4, rue Malher, Paris, 75004
Tel: 01 43 54 50 28	Tel: 01 42 72 40 21
Métro: Cardinal LeMoine or Jussieu	Métro: St Paul

Lunch

While *Europe Beyond Your Means* recommends doing activities other than eating on American Day, it is forgivable to consume enough during breakfast to have made yourself sick by lunchtime. The French are used to lighter lunches with more sensible portions. Take this opportunity to show them how it's actually done by stopping at one or more fast-food restaurants and gorging yourself until you nearly regurgitate. McDonald's is nearly mandatory at some point in the day, so this is an exceptional opportunity to give it a try, or look to other restaurants where you can order by number.

Pre-Dinner Drinks

After a long day suffering through some of the most intolerable food Paris has to offer, *Europe Beyond Your Means* suggests taking a small break before dinner with a touch of class. There is no better place to seriously celebrate the internationally exalted American spirit than the Hemmingway Bar at the Ritz. A smart and cozy bar located at the back of the famous hotel will remind you that not everything American is associated with hamburgers, fat people, or rock 'n' roll. *Europe Beyond Your Means* stresses the *back* of the hotel. Many guests think they are drinking in the so-called "Hemmingway Bar," but are really doing nothing more than ordering €40 drinks in the main bar at the front of the hotel. Unlike previous spots on your daylong journey, the Hemmingway Bar will apply a Ritz dress code. Thus, the ripped jeans, pocket flask, and peace symbol T-shirt you wore to visit Jim won't get you in the door at the Ritz. Be advised that the Hemmingway Bar has limited space, and it is not unusual to find a group waiting outside the door for a table to free up. Also, the bartenders here are world class, so don't feel at all bad about describing what it is you would like to taste in an ideal drink, and letting them do the rest. One of the many reasons it's now called the Hemmingway Bar is that the location is known for being the only place the famous author actually liberated during Operation Overlord. While the rest of the Allies were driving the Nazis out of Paris, Hem and his friends were alleged to have driven the Scotch from the bottle…but little else.

While the point of American Day is to be cliché, if the Hemmingway Bar is a little too canned for your tastes, try Harry's Bar. This establishment is also considered one of the world's most famous and best bars. Harry's may have a casual name, but it also has a flash of elegance and requires a similar dress code to the Ritz. Harry's Bar is of particular importance to American Day, as this spot is where the Bloody Mary was invented.

The Ritz – Hemmingway Bar	Harry's New York Bar
38, Rue Cambon	5 rue Daunou
75001	75002
Tel. +33.43.16.30.30	Tel. +33.42.61.71.14
Métro: Opéra or Concorde	Métro: Opéra

Dinner

As if you haven't already eaten enough, after breakfast, lunch, and likely a small snack, dinner could be the most important part of the day. The faint-hearted among your American legion will start to waiver, and dissenting comments such as "I just can't eat any more crap today" will start to frustrate your carefully laid-out plans. Few people outside of the Midwestern United States can spend a whole day consuming fried eggs, sausage, bacon, fried chicken, hoagies, pizza, and cheeseburgers without physical or emotional reservation. It is important at this point to have a *Beyond Your Means* leadership moment, and arrange the troops in proper formation. A motivating speech *à la* Knute Rockne may be in order; the real Notre Dame is, after all, right around the corner. You are most likely taking a group of out-of-shape food mercenaries into the hostile American dinnertime territory; therefore, a pep talk will probably be in order. Giving up or cutting the day short by heading to a café to get a salad makes you and your cadre nothing but quitters.

Europe Beyond Your Means has identified a few potential "hot spots" for American dining on this special day. While your authors have spent nearly this entire publication telling you to avoid these places like they are an econometrics course, it is now time to run headlong into them with great celebration. For an authentic experience, consider consulting the three wise men of American cuisine in Paris: The Hard Rock Café, Planet Hollywood, and T.G.I. Friday's.

There is no better way to celebrate Norman Rockwell than with grilled fajitas, pulled-pork sandwiches, bacon cheeseburgers, or world famous LA Lasagna. The force-fed culinary part of American Day is nearly over at this point, so feel free to indulge or at least test your constitution a little. The next day it will be back to croissants and sparkling water, if you even need to eat at all. Members of your group who are adamant about not eating any more unhealthy food for the day should easily be enticed by the "salads" that all three restaurants offer. Does anything say "healthy" more than a few leaves of romaine lettuce sprinkled with bacon bits and a healthy topping of boneless buffalo wings, swimming in blue-cheese dressing?

Hard Rock Café
14 Boulevard Montmartre
75009
Tel. +33.53.24.60.00
Métro: Richelieu-Drouot

Planet Hollywood
78 av. des Champs Elysees 75008
Tel. +33.53.83.78.27
Métro: Franklin D. Roosevelt or
Champs-Élysées-Clemenceau

T.G.I Friday's
8 Boulevard Montmartre
75009
Tel. +33.47.70.27.20
Métro: Richelieu-Drouot

Perhaps you cannot bring yourself to frequent the chain restaurants you abhor, both in America as well as abroad. We at *Europe Beyond Your Means* totally understand. As an alternative to visiting something plastic corporate and freakishly standard, you could also consider Joe Allen in Les Halles. While two Joe Allens exist in the United States, the best part about the Paris location is that it is American-themed. There are big-screen TVs for sporting events, cheese fries, and key lime pie on the menu, as well as the occasional Dixieland jazz band. If you happen to be in Paris during the American Independence Day, be sure to make reservations for Joe Allen's Fourth of July party.

Joe Allen
30 rue Pierre-Lescot
75001
Tel. +33.42.36.70.13
Métro: Étienne Marcel

There are so many examples of American culture in Paris that developing an itinerary to meet all of your needs and cure all of your cravings will prove very simple. Just remember that everything American that you want to do must be accomplished in one day; otherwise, your Parisian experience will not meet all of its potential.

11

Bidding Adieu

Even a *Beyond Your Means* traveler must eventually confront the inevitable reality and return to regular life away from Paris. This "regular life" can include anything from struggling student to perpetual vacationer to accountant with a wild side. But all will experience similar forms of separation anxiety from the life they temporarily lived while in Paris. It is difficult to leave behind the land of pretentious sophistication, the iconic monuments, and the three-foot-long baguettes, but it must be done. The following suggestions should help you return to your old life with minimal agitation:

Gradual Adaptation

Before departing Paris, ease back into your regular old lifestyle to provide a smooth transition. For example, if your chosen Parisian character is a European jet-setter, perhaps only sparing use of that Armani black pinstripe suit during your last week is in order. As much as this idea may offend your *faux* French sensibilities, remember that if your real life involves being an online insurance agent, whose only evening out every week involves breaded buffalo wings at Hooters, then sporting your Paris-character costume will be highly inappropriate.

Prepare Others

About two weeks before returning will be the time to start making amends. Many *Beyond Your Means* travelers may have hastily and dramatically quit their jobs prior to leaving for Paris. If you fall into said category, then this time is an exceptional opportunity to e-mail your former boss about how you used your trip as a reflection period and really hope there is still a spot in the "XYZ, Inc." family. Always be cognizant of the fact that if you are welcomed back, you may be forced to take a new analyst role under the management of Chapter 8's Executive Track Guy.

Since you might need someone to pick you up from the airport and listen to your tales, your steps 8 and 9 amends process of this particular recovery probably needs an expansion plan. Keep in mind that a long visit to France can be very much like alcoholism. Consider strategically placed phone calls to parents, friends, or other loved ones, emphatically conveying to them that this trip was exactly what you needed to grow up. Use empty yet reassuring statements like "I'm in a really good place right now" and "I just needed some time to reflect, and I realized that my old life was fine." Idle expressions like these will help you restore the social relationships you neglected by whimsically leaving in the first place. Always exploit the fact that others want you to mature.

Keep Up Foreign Relations

If you were on the extended-stay plan and followed *Europe Beyond Your Means* advice, then you probably subletted an apartment. Inevitably, you broke glasses, drank wine that you weren't supposed to, loaned out books that weren't yours, and generally created havoc in the bathroom. Never convince yourself that any of these (or that lamp or fan you broke during your first night) will go unnoticed. They won't. In order to prevent the owner of your temporary home from confirming any negative stereotypes about people from your home country, be sure to restore the apartment to its former state. You may have to go to the BHV and reluctantly replace broken items with better and more expensive ones. Trust us; there is no worse way to end your French fantasy than by receiving a harsh e-mail from an actual Parisian that labels you as all the stereotypes you tried so hard to escape, while threatening to withhold your deposit.

Taking these steps will assuredly help to alleviate many of the problems associated with your departure from *La République*.

Returning Home

Once the vacation is over, and you have deplaned somewhere much less exciting, your *Beyond Your Means* lifestyle and responsibilities do not have to end...necessarily. Sure, you will likely have to do something you detest to pay off your credit-card debt, but there are many ways to continue living the dream.

No matter what, the temptation to look and sound like a true Paris insider will be powerful, so only embrace it within reason. There is a certain preferred lexicon of the "been there, done that" crowd, so be sure to always adhere to certain rules when talking about your French experience. Remember to steer clear of exclamatory interjections like "When I lived in Paris" or "One time … in Paris" to avoid being labeled as the person who only talks about this one particular vacation. Your audience will tolerate stories and French references to an extent, so working within those limits will help you to maintain some form of credibility. Instead, consider these ideas for what is acceptable:

Referring to Favorite Things

It is completely acceptable to choose a few places or things from Paris to reference on occasion that you label as your "favorite." Close friends, however, will quickly tire of the hundred or so cafés, bistros, and brassieres now prodigiously labeled as your absolute "favorite." It is acceptable to mention your truly favorite bakery as much as you want, because this mitigates the potential for annoyance. After all, how many friends do you have who actually have a favorite bakery back home?

Conversely, everyone knows that French wine is famous; therefore, making a reference to your "favorite little vineyard that doesn't export" is not only acceptable but expected for any adventurer traveling under the *Beyond Your Means* banner. For example, a quaint vineyard in Vouvray named "Daniel Jarry" fits this exact description. If you didn't make it to any winery like this, surreptitiously substitute in *Le Clos Montmartre* instead. It is the only remaining vineyard in Paris and definitely does not export its miniscule amount of yield every year. However, keep the travel experience of your audience in mind if you are forced to go this route. The winery only produces about 1,700 half-liter bottles every year, and these are auctioned off for charity during an October wine festival. Therefore, this wine isn't only impossible to get outside of France, but it's also unavailable to the general public. Hence, there is a great risk of embarrassment if someone with knowledge on the subject calls your bluff.

Picking Up a Habit

It's completely fine to choose a French-inspired habit to incorporate into your daily life, which will not only be noticed but also garner envious attention. As long as the habit will not prove to be a social repellant to others, perform it at your leisure. For example, the French art of "complaining" is really only appreciated there, but a new and continuous addition of the luscious red lady in a stem glass at your daily meals will inspire others to privately discuss your new sophistication—provided that the wine doesn't lead you to becoming an utter inebriate.

Regaling Stories

Contrary to popular belief, others do love to hear your stories—at least, we think so. The art of storytelling is as complex as impressionistic art, but it can be boiled down to a few quick points.

Believability with Enhanced Quality

Yes, complete lies are tempting and more interesting than just about anything that actually happened, but an audience is really willing to accept only a few stories that seem a little outlandish. Consider the *Europe Beyond Your Means* Pareto Principle of storytelling: keep 80 percent of your facts true, while exaggerating them by 20 percent. This should keep everything relatively honest and believable, as well as interesting, but choose your more creative stories wisely, and limit their number.

Provided a story is based in truth, there is no reason not to elaborate. If you have a mediocre story, choosing to enhance it a little can easily take something that would otherwise be only mildly interesting and elevate it to one of your eccentric tales. For example, if you chose unwisely to visit a working girl in *Pigalle* who made you call her "princess," this can magically be translated into a secret rendezvous with deposed royalty.

Borrowing from Others

Beyond Your Means travelers all have a natural knack for storytelling. Sometimes in a group of other like-minded individuals, someone else will tell a much more classic anecdote than you have in your arsenal. While this can be cumbersome in the current social situation, just remember, when that individual isn't around, there is no reason to not borrow his story and claim it as your own. This can easily be justified for the sake of the story itself, since it was so good, it needed to be told as many times as possible.

Talking about a Romantic Interlude

Everyone craves details on foreign flings. Essentially, the female romance-novel market exists based on the idea of housewives being swept off of their feet by a European aristocrat. Likewise, every male has a secret French-maid fantasy. Basically, you have full license to discuss any romantic interludes you had in Paris with as many details as you want. Try and make the flings sound more mysteriously international than they really were. For example, the person drawing oversized head sketches for tourists outside the *Musée d'Orsay* can be transformed in your story to a new artist who paints in the style of Picasso and just opened a small gallery in Saint-Germain-des-Prés. Essentially, *Beyond Your Means* travelers should feel free to enhance their significant others' credentials as if they were their own résumés.

While there are acceptable means of drawing attention to your trip, it is important to avoid certain pitfalls that will only annoy friends and detract from your credibility. For example, some visitors to the land of *haute culture* don't always know when to let go after returning home—something especially endemic in *Beyond Your Means* travelers. This can result in both embarrassing and uncomfortable situations. Take, for instance, the female Francophile who returns to frigid Northern winters, defending herself with merely a silk scarf tied around her neck. Or consider the male adventurer, who after months in Paris, finally adopted the man-scarf into his wardrobe and wears one stateside at tailgates and dive bars. Unfortunately for him, the nicest insults hurled in his direction are inquiries asking if he's actually trying to dress like Fred from Scooby-Doo.

Temptations to Avoid

Below are temptations that should definitely be avoided after returning from a *Beyond Your Means* adventure in Paris.

Incorporating the French Language in Everyday Conversation

Some former tourists persist on doing really irritating things, like working French into a conversation—*long* after they've returned from Paris. Greeting a friend or colleague with "*Bonjour*" and a sly smile is fine the first week or so after returning, as long as that person knew you were adventuring for an extended period. But keeping up the charade long afterward only makes you look childish. More annoying still are the travelers who will "inadvertently" hop into French during a conversation and coyly wait until the other participants in the discussion deliver blank looks in their direction. These "accidental speakers" then mutter something like, "Oh, I've been speaking

French so long that I didn't realize I was doing it." There is absolutely no truth to this myth. It takes about ten minutes at customs to revert back to the mother tongue. More likely, it only takes the plane ride home to realize you don't have to stumble through French anymore. Keeping up the act for a couple of weeks after a trip will only perturb everyone around you.

Talking about How Different Everything Is in France

Another bothersome quirk that *Beyond Your Means* travelers should avoid after returning home is acting surprised by incessantly pointing out that things aren't like they were in France. Not every restaurant brings free bread before the meal starts, serves cheese for dessert, or allows you to occupy a table for hours while engaging in conversation. Meeting up with friends at Denny's for Sunday brunch does not give anyone the license to act surprised by the extra-large portions or the rapid table service. However, for *Beyond Your Means* travelers, this may provide the perfect cover for accidentally omitting a tip after too much time spending money that they didn't have while away. Note that this cute side trick is only allowed after a significant time abroad, so don't abuse it.

Posting Pictures on the Internet

This is a general travel rule but can particularly be applied to *Beyond Your Means* travelers. There are a variety of Web sites that specialize in letting others look at your exotic vacations, but travelers must accept that people just don't care. Despite e-mails that say "Just saw your pics; it looks like you had a blast!" people don't actually look through your album unless they think there might be a picture of them in it—or a naked photo of someone other than you. Refraining from this exercise is advised.

Over-Romanticizing Your Trip

Odds are, your visit to France lasted only a few months, at the most. There is no need to act like the trip was completely life-altering and opened your eyes to so many new things. You are not, all of a sudden, a Socialist, a food connoisseur, a poet, or a painter just because you took a vacation. Barring an unplanned religious epiphany at *Sacré-Cœur*, basically, nothing should change in your life.

Brand New Perspectives

In the same vein as not over-romanticizing your trip, do not adopt new views on life simply because of a really fun holiday. It is more than likely that you didn't engage in much conversation with the French themselves, so using your three-week vacation as an opportunity to showcase great enlightenment on new political issues is silly.

Using Canned Sayings

American visitors to Europe are famous for returning home and saying outlandish things like "I just can't drink American beer anymore; it tastes like water!" Yes, European beers are exponentially more flavorful, but you are going to have to taste the Rockies eventually. Sooner or later, you may find yourself in a situation where keg stands are required, and the hosts of that party probably didn't splurge on *La Bavaisienne*. Other popular post-France phrases include stating the obvious, like "You know, in France they have wine with every meal," and the classic "Getting around Europe is just so easy." *Beyond Your Means* has developed an official academic position on statements like this: Ugh.

Instead, one should seek out more original canned sayings like "I really prefer the detachable shower heads that are standard in Paris and am thinking of installing one in my apartment, since I don't have room for a *bidet*," or "The deodorant they have over there is just so effective. I wonder why they don't use it?" Lines like these will signal to others the true depth of your cultural experience, as well as project humor that even a provincial audience can appreciate.

Staying in Character

As advised earlier, your trip to Paris is the perfect time to adopt a new persona to use. Sadly, however, this character must be abandoned once stepping on the plane to return home. This is important for two reasons: First, there is no need to let your friends at home realize just how far you have truly strayed from the flock. And second, it is likely that your character will in no way fit the role you play at home. You can be a hipster in Paris, but it's a lot harder in Louisville.

Discussing Plans for Another *Beyond Your Means* Adventure

There is no question that you will be taking other *Beyond Your Means* adventures at some point, but you might have told people that this was the last "big trip." Alternatively, you might purport the idea that you have finally grown up and are now ready to settle down. Therefore, *Beyond Your Means* recommends taking at least three months before discussing another trip publicly. It will be difficult to be taken seriously in any aspect of your life if you start discussing another irresponsible trip only days after you stepped off the plane from your "one last hurrah." Granted, it's perfectly fine for *Beyond Your Means* travelers to immediately start planning and strategizing the second they get home; just keep the plans to yourself for a while.

Writing a Travel Guide

Sorry. The market has been cornered.

Your trip to Paris is supposed to be one of the most exciting and *Beyond Your Means* that you ever take. Adjusting to life back home will be difficult, but it is essential to remember these suggestions. By following these points, you will be more readily accepted by those who stayed behind and can then begin plotting your next adventure to another *Beyond Your Means* city.

Afterword

In 1915 the French Army took to the field of battle wearing their version of Nantucket Reds (*le pantalon rouge*) and bright blue jackets. This was a conscious decision. Ostensibly, the French Army could not be asked to suffer the fashion embarrassment of the new muted gray and blue uniforms adopted by both their adversaries and allies during the early twentieth century. The French soon found themselves at a massive disadvantage. Since this was not the most tactical policy to win the war, they were eventually forced to change their uniforms to the same drab colors that many of the other nations were wearing. Hey, at least the French Army had arrived at the party with the most style—that kind of entrance can never be taken away from them.

While the above anecdote is factually accurate, it is often used as a humorous story to mock the French for their poor planning, unabashed resistance to change what had worked in the past, and their unmitigated commitment to fashion. Perhaps the French hadn't considered adapting because this stratagem had won many wars for them in the past, or perhaps it was that style is such a paradigm for the nation. Whatever the reason, this glimpse at history provides a look into the essence of France in the way that giving a knock-off Statue of Liberty as a gift provides strong commentary on the United States.

The French often get a bad rap and are subject to criticism for their views and approach to just about everything. Basically, France is unapologetically different from the rest of the occidental world and shows no desire to fall in with the herd. Things like fighting a well-dressed war or the fashion show that was their recent presidential election illustrate the entertaining quirks that others are quick to criticize. But on a more serious note, France offers so much to the world that cannot be discounted simply because they do everything in "fun colors" with well-placed accessories. French citizens seem to always provide the world with just enough *lagniappe* to keep things interesting. The nation is an interesting mix of contrasts; their diplomacy is as legendary as their extremism.

Europe Beyond Your Means has matured past the point of feeling petty jealousy toward the French or trying to sarcastically point out what's wrong with their culture. Perhaps the French are right. How else do you explain the fact that France has been able to give the proverbial middle finger to nearly every country in the world at one time or another, but we all keep coming back to them, like a dedicated yet unappreciated lover. Referring back to the world characters in their high-school roles, all the boys want to date France, but her aloof and invidious attitude leads to resentment. There is something undeniably sexy about everything the French are and stand for.

Understanding the French and self-reflection on Anglophone culture is only part of the dual goals of this publication. The other, of course, is to grant travelers permission to go through this process in the most comprehensive way possible. To truly learn a culture and experience what should be gained through travel cannot be done superficially. Essentially, when the urge hits to travel the world for the sake of nothing more than the intrinsic value, look to *Europe Beyond Your Means* as giving you the approval that no one else can.

So, discard the preconceived notions and traditional methods of travel and seek out Paris ... *Beyond Your Means. Bon voyage!*

Acknowledgments

Michelle Holman and Jenn Ziemann for editorial assistance

Special Thanks

CC's Coffee House in New Orleans for the endless refills, the Vanderbilt University Student Center for the space, and the Cornell Club of New York City for the free Diet Coke.

Conrad—Conrae Lucas-Adkins and "the Rowdies"
William—Matthew Norgard and Iain Balmain (especially for financial and emotional support in London)

Index

About the Authors

Conrad G. Lucas II

Born in the mountains of West Virginia, Conrad Gale Lucas II considers himself a writer, academic, lawyer, politico, and part-time anything else. He has worked in every environment from education to big tobacco and holds a bachelor's degree from Vanderbilt (where he is also working on a doctorate in his spare time), a master's degree from Harvard, and a law degree from Tulane. A lifelong Francophile, he earned a certificate in international law at *La Sorbonne*. He currently practices law in West Virginia but at any given moment could be in Nashville, New Orleans, Oxford, Mississippi, or anywhere else in the American South, depending on his mood. Never one to let moss grow under his feet, he is always planning his next European adventure.

William D. Norgard

William D. Norgard was born in the rustbelt in the late 1970s and spent his formative years in Cleveland, Ohio. Later, he attended Cornell University, obtaining a bachelor's degree in history, then worked for several years in London and New York as a banker and consultant, respectively. Later, he returned to the United States to attend Cardozo Law School. It was during those years that he took opportunities to internationally enhance his tradecraft at *Sorbonne-Paris I*. Often returning to Europe a few times a year, he frequently makes Paris a stopover if there is anyway to rationalize it. He now resides in New York City, helps manage the family farm in Kansas, and is looking for something meaningful to do but would prefer to continue writing and traveling.

Manufactured By: RR Donnelley
Breinigsville, PA USA
April 2010